002150

Wild Strawberries (1957), Ingmar Bergman

IMAGES OF MAN

a critique of the contemporary cinema

donald j. drew

InterVarsity Press
Downers Grove
Illinois 60515

InterVarsity Press is the
book publishing division of
Inter-Varsity Christian Fellowship.

"The Conclusion" by
Steve Turner is reprinted by
kind permission of Charisma Books
37 Soho Square, London W1.

Photo credits: The film stills in
this book were secured
through the assistance of
the National Screen Service
Corporation, Chicago, and
reproduced with their permission.

ISBN 0-87784-482-8
Library of Congress Catalog
Card Number: 74-20099

Printed in the United
States of America

The Pawnbroker (1965), Sidney Lumet

contents

preface

It is tempting to think that the cinema leads today's cultural consensus. The cinema is a weathervane pointing to the postulates and lifestyles which surround and subsume us all, even though most of us most of the time are oblivious to them. Of course, other mass media also herald shifts in cultural ideas. Since the paperback revolution the novel has become especially popular. Magazines and weeklies have increased enormously in variety and circulation. Pop and rock groups command a vast following, and there is considerable interest in classical music. The art world, drama, sculpture, ballet, architecture and manifold arts and crafts flourish and involve increasing numbers of devotees. Advertisements too have a colossal influence on the minds and money of the public. Polyphemus, the one-eyed TV monster, has a foot in both camps of media and message, perhaps to a larger extent than most other cultural activities. Yet cinema—linked with but stronger in its influence and more forceful in its thrust than TV—is, I believe, leading today's cultural consensus.

Each of the arts or cultural activities within a society both reflects and promotes its own thought-forms and lifestyles. Each not only proclaims a message but is as much one of the media as the newspaper or radio. Yet with the uniqueness each art brings to the cultural scene, there is a common philosophic link between them. The paintings of de Chirico find a parallel in the music of Stockhausen and a counterpart in the plays of Peter Handke. A culturewide interest in the various arts helps to obliterate the artificial distinction between classes and ages. In brief, cultural activities reflect and promote thought-forms and lifestyles; there is a common philosophical link between them; they are available to all.

But the cinema, I think, leads the cultural consensus. In this book, I want to develop this thesis, show the postulates from which directors are working, examine some answers they are giving to man's current search for meaning and finally consider some criteria for judging films and finding a viable world view. In doing so, I hope to be neither negative nor alarmist. There is distinction in film as an art form and pleasure in cinema-viewing as an experience. I hope in what follows to convey something of that pleasure.

acknowledgments

In addition to attending scores of films over the past twenty years, recently with note pad and pen handy, I have consulted countless film reviews, scripts and interviews with actors and directors. Among the journals whose reviews I have found consistently helpful are *Time, Newsweek, The Times* (London), *The Daily Telegraph* (London), *The Observer* (London), *The Guardian* (Manchester and London) and *Right On.*

If I have failed to acknowledge the source of some review or some peculiarly apt insight or turn of phrase, this is not intentional, and my sincere apologies are due in advance.

In his poem "Ulysses," Tennyson makes the ancient hero say, "I am part of all that I have met," and with this I can identify because this book owes so much to so many people. It derives a great deal from the community and cultural environment in which I lived for a number of happy and fulfilled years and in particular from Gini who suggested it and Os and Jenny who encouraged it. My thanks are due also to Dr. James Sire, Editor of IVP, for the invitation to write this book and for his courtesy, forbearance and exhortation.

Finally, a word of appreciation and gratitude is owed to my large and loved family of friends and students who listened, criticized and urged me towards the printing press.

All these may take some credit for the "perfections." The imperfections are mine.

Donald J. Drew

The Virgin Spring (1960), Ingmar Bergman   *Two English Girls* (1972), Francois Truffaut

film as art

1

Because film conforms basically to principles that are observed in other arts, film may be said to be an art form. In fact, if we exclude TV, it is the only major art form to have appeared this century. In film, knowledge, skill and dexterity are applied to an aesthetic expression of language, action and emotion through the medium of words, sounds and colors. What more could be required of an art form?

Still, we must ask: What is the purpose of an art form? I would contend that its basic purpose is to define and redefine man. A painting by Rembrandt and one by Francis Bacon, for example, define and redefine man as he is seen from age to age; each is different yet each reflects something of what is there. In other words, through art men try to understand and to communicate the meaning of life.

Throughout the centuries there has been a variety of views on the nature of art. To recall some of these will put my own view in perspective. Walter Pater saw the artist as a liberator of his raw materials. Henry James saw art as "all discrimination and selection." Herbert Read speaks of it as "emotion cultivating good form" leading eventually to harmony. In other words, the artist takes his raw materials—clay, words, photographic images—and from them fashions artistic objects.

But the major view with which I am in sympathy is that art consists in reproducing or imitating real life and thus more clearly shows us the intrinsic nature of some things than we would otherwise see. Keats, for one, thought beauty was tantamount to truth and that art was essentially a search for truth. Shakespeare in *Hamlet* stated the purpose of drama to be to hold "the mirror up to nature . . . to show . . . the very age and body of the time his form and pressure [character]." This same idea is taken up by Stendahl who remarked that "a novel is a mirror carried along a roadway." In more recent times, I. A. Richards spoke of art as "the supreme form of communicative activity." And D. W. Griffith, an outstanding early American film director, wrote: "The task I am trying to achieve is to make you see." The film, he thought, should be a person's eye. But Francois Truffaut goes further, for in a recent interview he **14** commented that "cinema is an improvement on life."

According to these views, then, the arts reveal the human condition and define and redefine man in his multifarious activities and relationships. Yet to do this, a paradox seems to be required: To see a thing as it is intrinsically, we must view it as something else. In other words, we can see ourselves only if we see a reflection of ourselves. What a long way we have come since Miracle, Morality and Mystery plays were performed on carts in medieval inn yards! There the art was confined to the carts but influenced the life. Art imitated life. Today, art forms not only reflect and promote thought-forms and lifestyles but, Byron-like, tend to become life itself.

From such considerations emerge three characteristics of art: (1) the artist's intuition, experience and perception, (2) the expression of these in an artistic medium and (3) the appreciation of the end result by others. Art is thus related to reality. The artist, because he lives in a real world, is able to draw from it valid and meaningful inspiration and relate this to a suitable artistic medium in such a way that other people, also living in a real world, may be able to appreciate what he is doing.

It becomes obvious, therefore, that film is an art form in its own right. An artist (a director) by means of mechanical devices (cameras and sound equipment) sets out to create a film world that is false objectively but which succeeds in giving the viewer, through a "willing suspension of disbelief," the illusion of reality.[1] If the art fails to create the illusion of "seeming," then it is only a gimmick, only what an enterprising showman in a late nineteenth-century French fair hailed as a *Lenti-Electro-Plasti-Chromo-Mimo-Poly-Serpentigraf!* A film that does not fail to create the illusion of "seeming" is Truffaut's *Day for Night,* a film about a film maker watching a film maker making a film, which is not only first-rate entertainment but instructive and constructive concerning the art of the film.

stage and screen

Tennessee Williams has commented that the film is "better for exploring the mid-century obsession. They [the directors] have suddenly discovered how to use the camera to suggest things the stage can't. It's more penetrating, the poetry of suggestion. . . . These subtle changes they can give in close-ups of faces." In other words, a film is not a cinematic version of a novel or a play. In addition to the interpretative view of the director, film applies its own distinctive techniques. That is why a film version of a novel or a play has to be different from the original if the film is to stand as an art form that defines man and reflects what is there to be seen.

From its earliest days, the cinema has implemented Tennessee Williams' observations; silent films relied heavily on close-ups of faces, and technological advance augmented the effect of this. In *Satyricon,* evil and grotesque as many of the faces are, Fellini makes them speak in epic proportions. "Faces are my words," he says. Bergman pays close attention to faces and the stories they tell as *Virgin Spring* among others indicates. An actor on the stage is not subjected to this attention but seeks rather to convey his whole personality to the audience; there is much more of a person-to-person approach. In Bresson's film, *Mouchette,* however, words are cut to a minimum, while in *Death in Venice* Visconti has produced a film remarkable for its lack of dialogue, for his intention was specifically

15

"to lose words as far as possible." Bergman's *Silence* and *Cries and Whispers* are soundless much of the time, but this in itself conveys meaning. Long periods of silence are used by Pasolini in *The Gospel according to St. Matthew*. The point is: The film is different from the novel (which, without words, disappears) or the drama (which, without words, becomes pantomime).

A contemporary film can achieve an instant, almost subliminal, effect on the viewer through the use of technical devices not available to the stage producer. Close-ups; refraining from a close-up when one has been led to anticipate it; zooming (Hitchcock in *The Birds* uses this adroitly); rapid motion; slow motion; freezing; exact framing; panning; dollying; juxtaposition of images; parallel images; superimposed images; surreal images; flashbacks; the use of mirrors; static camera making tracking shots prominent; the use of different lenses (Kubrick's *A Clockwork Orange* brilliantly employs the fish-eye lens and other devices); variety of lighting; dressing up the sound track with music, sounds and voices—all of these both comment on the action and amplify a film's philosophic statement. Such resources are not at the disposal of a producer of stage plays; here a more rapid and immediate rapport between actor and audience is required. In *Superfly* the close-ups of Priest and his paramour making love in the bath would be ineffective if not impossible on the stage.

The French film director, Robert Bresson, has written of his work,

> Acting is for the theater, which is a bastard art. The film can be a true art because in it the author takes fragments of reality and arranges them in such a way that their juxtaposition transforms them. Art *is* transformation. Each shot is like a word, which means nothing by itself, or rather means so many things that in effect it is meaningless. But a word in a poem is transformed, its meaning made precise and unique, by its placing in relation to the words around it; in the same way a shot in a film is given its meaning by its context, and each shot modifies the meaning of the previous one until with the last shot a total, unparaphraseable meaning has been arrived at. Acting has

nothing to do with that, it can only get in the way. Films are
made only by by-passing the will of those who appear in them,
using not what they do but what they are.[2]

Some years ago a director remarked, "It doesn't matter about the
script. I've got the camera." These statements accentuate the difference between film and drama insofar as film claims to be a distinct art form.

Those involved in the production of a film must surrender themselves to the will of the director. To a large extent, this is Bergman's
position: He thinks through what he wants to portray, writes the
script, produces the film, directs it, demands total control and total
obedience. He is a benevolent despot, rightly ruthless in preventing
anyone or anything from jeopardizing his building of the film as he
sees it. The team of actors, actresses and technicians with whom he
has worked over the years testify to their loyalty to him and to the
single-mindedness and success of his art. Each first-rate director requires the same surrender and commitment. Truffaut, like Bergman, may be considered not only a director but an innovator, a   **17**
"director-as-artist," single-mindedly and sensitively focusing on
"humanness." So also no doubt was Shakespeare who also was script
writer, actor, producer and manager, at the heart of the commercial theater of his day which was, as with film, a group enterprise.

In his introduction to the script of *Wild Strawberries,* Bergman in
1957 wrote,

> Cinematography is based on deception of the human eye. I've
> worked it out that if I see a film which has a running time of
> one hour, I sit through twenty-five minutes of complete dark-
> ness—the blankness between the frames. When I show a film,
> I am guilty of deceit. I use an apparatus which is constructed
> to take advantage of a certain human weakness, an apparatus
> with which I can sway my audience in a highly emotional man-
> ner—make them laugh, scream with fright, smile, believe in
> fairy stories, become indignant, feel shocked, charmed, deeply
> moved or perhaps yawn with boredom.[3]

This at once places cinema in a class of its own; there is no case for
asserting that a film is a cinematic version of a novel or a play.

In an interview not long ago Bergman captured the distinctions between theater and cinema. He reflected that in the theater we see real flesh and blood speaking and acting out their lives. They do so irrespective of us, the audience; they do not know us but they know each other; they can keep to their separate identities or share them among themselves. We have little contact with them or they with us, and when the evening is over they return to their homes, we to ours. In the cinema it is different. One enters, as it were, incognito. Unlike the theater, there is no special sense of occasion, no reserved seat for you alongside someone you know. In the cinema it is dark; you can sit where you like; you can settle down into your own dreams. You could be anybody, and if you could be anybody then no one else knows what you are looking at and what your dreams really are.

In other words, we watch TV to see anything; we go to the theater to see and to be seen; but we go to the cinema to see and remain unknown. There we can dream our dreams before, during and after the film, and, as the song in "Joseph and the Amazing Technicolor Dream Coat" says, "Any dream will do."

the camera does the acting

To what extent Bergman would agree with Bresson that "theater is a bastard art," I do not know, but it is not difficult to see the wide gulf between theater and cinema and the factors which create and contribute to it.[4]

In cinema, the camera has two eyes. First, it is the eye of the director, establishing the association the viewer is going to have with the images. In practice, the eye of the director and the eye of the viewer are one, for what the director wants me to see I have to see. Second, the camera is the eye of the character in the film. Not only does the director guide the viewer to see the character or what the character sees, but he establishes the character's own point of view through the camera. The subjective consciousness of the character is thus revealed through a technique parallel to the stream-of-consciousness technique used sometimes in contemporary novels.

Essentially the camera does the acting; it is almost as if the actor-

Oh! What a Lovely War (1969), Richard Attenborough

pawn is moved by the camera-player.[5] The viewer moves with the camera because he sees through the eye of the camera. He does not interact with actors but with images, and this psychic distance has a dynamic effect on him. One second he sees a figure in the far distance; the next second he sees the texture of that figure's sensuous lips.

Film is ideally suited to identification of viewer with actor or situation. Because of the angle of the camera, the viewer is repeatedly being compelled to adopt different roles, alternating between observer, participant and voyeur. The viewer can see not only from viewpoints that no one who was not actually present could see from; he can see not only through keyholes but under bedclothes. All this is determined for him by the camera.

In the theater, actors act on a stage that separates them from the audience, and the psychic distance is a known quantity. In the cinema, however, psychic distance is an unknown quantity. The effect of darkness, plus the frequent visual devices, makes it both unknown and fluctuating, and one result of this is that the viewer, although observing only images on a screen, seems to feel that those images are more real than actors on a stage.

In the theater, the viewer has at least the illusion that all five senses are being employed, but in the cinema he knows that they are restricted—at the moment—to two, sight and sound. Through the eye of the camera he is viewing a two-dimensional picture of a three-dimensional world. The camera, aiming to present reality, leads and misleads, and in next to no time the distinction between illusion and reality may be clouded. For example, the use of slow motion prevents one from asserting that only reality is presented on the screen. The aim essentially is to present reality, but one must beware of a blanket proposition to this effect, for in this instance, as in others, the camera misleads. In fact, images, whether of man or otherwise, often supplant reality. And from time to time visual images and sound track are unsynchronized; they function independently and may convey separate ideas.

The bravura of the social satire in Bunuel's *The Discreet Charm of the Bourgeoisie* does not obscure the frequent confusion of illusion and reality. Not surprisingly, dreams play a notable part, one character saying, "Sometimes dreams are really . . ." and "I dreamed that Senechal dreamed."[6]

The world of dreams, given a Freudian emphasis, frequently features in modern cinema, usually in terms of the current confusion between reality and illusion as *Last Year in Marienbad, Belle de Jour, Blow-Up* and *Juliet of the Spirits* reveal. What is real and what is illusory? And consequently, What is true and what is false? These are among several crucial questions raised by films of this kind. Such films take us into the area of present Underground Films and far beyond Blake's "As for me, I prefer the world of dreams; straight past the northern star will do."

Much of today's film, whether in the cinema or on TV, blurs the sharp edge between reality and illusion. This is, of course, particularly the case with the "surrealists." In the first place, the technological devices being employed help to convey a subjective view of reality through a close identification with, and even manipulation of, the viewer. Second, this subjective view of reality is augmented by the often illusory and distorted world of the soap operas, a world so frequently presented that it, too, tends to be seen as reality.

film comes of age

The early film makers had some idea of the potential available to them in the cinematograph. What they may not have foreseen is that the cinema has achieved a status among the arts and a position of power in the media that places it in the vanguard of other art forms. From D. W. Griffith to Stanley Kubrick is a mere sixty years (although the first motion picture appeared in 1895 and the cinematograph was thought of as a vulgar, fairground attraction), and yet it has been a period of the most rapid technological and philosophical change in man's history.

Apart from a few distinguished films such as Griffith's *Intolerance* or Eisenstein's *Battleship Potemkin,* the stock in trade of the early cinema was cops and robbers, the superb and often satirical comedies of Mack Sennet, Charlie Chaplin, Laurel and Hardy, Harold Lloyd and others, interspersed with sentimental romances. A middle period evolved, with more sentimentalism (acted out by stars such as Charles Boyer, Greta Garbo and Clark Gable) mixed with westerns, new style cops and robbers, thrillers, and a new genre, the 21 animated cartoon. Post-1945 film evolution has dressed up most of the old mutton as lamb and added the documentary, educational, horror, avant-garde, sub-cult, pornographic and "underground" film. Thus in sixty years the cinema has not only evolved from a happy-go-lucky investment by small-time entrepreneurs to the Mogul empire of MGM, but its entire ethos has undergone a monumental metamorphosis. What was a gamble with public taste now has a strong position as a major art form.

Some years ago a film critic observed, "It would not be surprising if films in the future divided themselves more sharply into two classes, the serious and the popular, and these classes themselves became more and more distinct from one another." Apart from "serious" and "popular" begging the question, that prophecy has largely come true, even though in the process a matter of social concern such as war (as portrayed in *Journey's End* or *All Quiet on the Western Front*) is treated quite differently today (witness *Paths of Glory* and *Oh! What a Lovely War*). Moreover, the contribution of commercial film to the entertainment industry is not all in terms of avant-garde films; the proportion is probably one "popular" to two avant-garde. But a random selection of recent "populars," those that are straightforward or comparatively innocuous, gives us the following: *Around the World in Eighty Days, The Red Balloon, Those Magnificent Men in Their Flying Machines, The Battle of Britain, Traffic, Cromwell, The Lion in Winter, Anne of a Thousand Days, Airport, When Eight Bells Toll, Bullitt, Fiddler on the Roof, Playtime, Young Winston, Kes, Lawrence of Arabia, Sounder, Conrack, The Three Musketeers.* This somewhat arbitrary list gives some indication that the film industry's menu spans the gap between McDonald's hamburgers and Maxim's of Paris.

the camera as a fountain pen

The present position of the film on both sides of the Atlantic (and this book confines itself to films available in English-speaking versions) is unambiguously stated by Alexandre Astruc who sees the camera as a *Caméra Stylo,* a fountain pen. He writes,

This image has a very precise sense. It means that the cinema will break away little by little from the tyranny of the visual, of the image for its own sake, of the immediate anecdote, of the concrete, to become a means of writing as supple and as subtle as that of written language. No area must be barred to it. The most austere meditation, attitudes to all human works, psychology, metaphysics, ideas, passions are very precisely its province. Indeed, these ideas and visions of the world are such that today the cinema alone is capable of giving them full realization.[7]

This is a bold but not pretentious claim firmly to establish the cinema as the leading art form and is in line with the observations of Tennessee Williams, Robert Bresson and Ingmar Bergman. It states precisely the point at which the industry in the main has arrived.

Consider, for example, the fine calligraphy of Bunuel's *The Discreet Charm of the Bourgeoisie.* Bunuel's direction is indeed supple and subtle; he captures the nuances, the ironic shades in meaning, feelings and opinions in people and circumstances. The subtlety of a Conrad or the irony of a Flaubert is transposed to the screen. By the same token, Francois Truffaut's *Two English Girls* is etched with a combination of naturalness and delicacy.

The same overall principles are at work in Visconti's elegant *Death in Venice,* where he choreographs the sartorial niceties and studied nonchalance of the monied classes in a luxurious hotel. But the spotlight is on the problem of the relationship between Aschenbach and Tadzio, on the part of the former a relationship of suffering silence and on the part of the latter a teasing, silent innuendo. The camera has selected not "the tyranny of the visual, of the image for its own sake," but the inner levels of consciousness. This is observed also in Aschenbach's metaphysical problem: Is perfection the important thing in creativity? Should the artist create ugliness because that too is a part of life? Aschenbach struggles with these problems and breaks down, well aware of his own decadent nature. The film is a splendid illustration of "the poetry of suggestion."

A film that does not see the camera as a fountain pen in quite the same way as Visconti's is *Satyricon.* It would appear that Fellini in this film has not broken away from "the tyranny of the visual, of the image for its own sake, of the immediate anecdote, of the concrete," for the viewer from the start is seized by the scruff of the neck and frog-marched from one grotesque or savage or voluptuous episode to another. Fellini brilliantly opens up for us ancient Rome in all its paganism and superstition, dedicated to sensuous satisfactions and the acquisition of wealth. The dreary decadence and search for satisfaction in hedonism is epitomized in Encolpius' amoral indecision and the anguish of his loneliness as he moves about in a society without moral sanctions, personal friendship or collective responsibility. Rome then was in an advanced state of moral and political decay, and the film fixes on one of the results of disseminated decadence: The characters are seen not so much as persons but as a part of the Jungian concept of the flow of consciousness in which humanness itself tends to evaporate. A parallel between then and now can hardly be avoided, and the dictum of distinguished anthropologist J. D. Unwin is underscored: "Any human society is free to choose either to display great energy or to enjoy sexual freedom. The evidence is that it cannot do both for more than one generation."

Films like *A Clockwork Orange* and *O Lucky Man!* although using the camera as a *Caméra Stylo,* have yet retained "the tyranny of the visual" because of the savage images. But to the extent that the visual is not exclusive or used for its own sake, it need not be tyrannous. Today's directors are developing and taking full advantage of the cornucopia of technical devices available to them. As Astruc says, "No area must be barred to it," and no area is barred to the *Caméra Stylo.*

Yet perhaps equal in importance to the camera is the editing of the film, and committed directors spend a large portion of their total time on this work of selection. Certain takes are chosen, others omitted, others added, others re-taken on the set or location. The revised takes then are projected for further criticism. This is a meticulous and prolonged piece of work that a conscientious director will assign only to himself. From time to time he may even become his own camera man, knowing that his insight of the moment can be captured only by himself. "Once the camera is running," said Bertolucci in a recent interview, "it is only I who move it. No one else can touch it because it represents my presence in the film, allowing me to mingle with my actors."

Film is a part of the entertainment industry and inseparable from big business. But it is still an art form, and one can admire the skill, artistry, intelligence and integrity that a dedicated and sensitive director and his team bring to their work and to the screen.

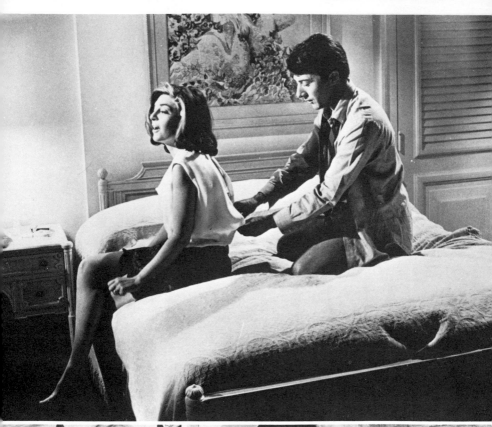

The Graduate (1967), Mike Nichols   *The Ruling Class* (1972), Peter Medak

the cultural consensus

2L

We live in a time of accelerating and exciting change; every area of our lives is affected. Writing in the early years of the nineteenth century, Jane Austen made no reference to Britain's mammoth struggle with Napoleon. One reason is that the war scarcely affected the life of the man in the street. How different was the Second World War! Today, because of the technological revolution in communication, Jane Austen's perspective is impossible. Through the influence of the media we are subjected sometimes to infiltration, sometimes to bombardment, by concepts and values formerly undreamt of.

Who, even a few years ago, would have imagined that some statesmen and businessmen would consult horoscopes in order to determine their policies, or that the occult in its different expressions would be so prevalent? Who would have imagined that we would so disturb the balance of nature as to threaten even our survival; or that sex festivals would become as common as country fairs; or that a distinguished psychologist would assert that "to man *qua* man we readily say good riddance"; or that a responsible psychiatrist would maintain that madness is not illness but a transcendent experience above that of so-called normal people? The cultural force these random illustrations represent penetrates deeply into the social mores and the personal living of thousands of people. Millions who are not affected by nor involved in any of these or more bizarre activities are nonetheless subject to the prevailing thought-forms and to some degree to the resultant lifestyles.

the relativity of nearly everything

Sixty years ago, directors could make films on the generally accepted basis that the moral concepts of right and wrong existed and that if one thing was right, its opposite was wrong. The phrase *goodies and baddies* that described one type of film makes this clear. There was, moreover, an unwritten code that stated that at least by the end of the film, vice must be punished and virtue rewarded.

As fresh thinking distilled in various academic disciplines, in particular those of the behavioral sciences and theology, and as these ideas percolated down to the supermarket level, the former moral concepts tended to be played down; man came to be viewed as being caught somewhere between Pavlov's conditioned reflexes and Freud's subconscious.[1] Words like *choice, volition* and *purpose* were replaced by *determined, chance* and *alienation,* and film directors tried to divert this mood into a frantic jazz beat of escapism. Since the Second World War, philosophically the moral concepts have largely vanished, and the dance-your-troubles-away mood of the 20s and 30s has been superseded by the notion of do-your-own-thing, while alienation has shadowed into despair.

Now each of the arts reflects and in turn promotes today's thought-forms and resulting lifestyles. Allen Ginsberg's poems, Francis Bacon's paintings, John Cage's music, Henry Moore's sculptures, Bob Dylan's songs, Kurt Vonnegut's novels have the same philosophical thread running through them. But it does not stop at that level. Through the incessant multiplicity of newspaper and magazine articles and popular radio and TV programs, these postulates have filtered down from the university to the supermarket level.

What are the thought-forms or postulates on which film directors are working? Stimulated by the enervating effect of the materialistic doctrine of "the good life" and suffering from an exaggerated sense of post-colonial guilt which led to excessive liberalization, a minority of "progressives" were able to capture and control much of the media. They are the ones largely responsible for introducing to-day's open, permissive and iconoclastic lifestyle. However, this was the occasion rather than the cause, for the concept of *absolute* or *objective truth* had long been abandoned.

This is the primary postulate: Truth, if it matters at all, is something that is subjective and relative; it is a matter of opinion from individual to individual and shifts from situation to situation. The viewpoint expressed in Yeats' poem "A Vision" sums it up: "I make the truth." The antithesis of something being true and therefore something else being false, of something being right and therefore something else being wrong, has been jettisoned. There remains only the large against the small, the infinite against the finite. What used to be considered evil is now reckoned to be mystery or complexity. In such a climate of thought, self-affirmation or self-authentication becomes an end in itself, and even the concept of a social contract is ignored.

It is important to note that there is no such thing as absolute or objective truth because there is no such person as the God described in the Bible. God is dead. Dostoevsky expressed it this way: "If there is no God, then everything is permitted." Because of the commitment to subjectivism and relativism, the concept of morality has to disappear, and when that goes, the concept of normality soon follows it.[2]

But at this point modern man is caught. He has denied the existence of a God of absolute truth, and with that he has eliminated the ground for morality and eventually normality. Yet he still has to live in a real world, and he still has to account for his inner motions as a man. So at this point two divergent theses concerning the nature of man arise: Either man is seen to be determined chemically and psychologically (which implies that he is a piece of machinery and open to manipulation),[3] or he is doomed to be free and at the same time master of his fate because he himself is at the core of the cosmos.[4]

29

Yet modern man can live with neither of these alternatives.

Because of what he intrinsically *is* in the real world and in himself, he is in a position of unbearable tension and falls into a state of despair. Often he opts for nihilism which he tends to grasp as a proper, adult attitude to life. But nihilism, if taken seriously, leads to a denial of the reality of all existence. In nihilism there is only silence and alienation, and no man can bear this for long. One cannot live long in a world of emptiness, and the professor who is "spreading futility" in *Butley* shows this well.

Samuel Beckett asks, "How am I, an a-temporal being imprisoned in time and space, to escape from my imprisonment when I know that outside time and space lies Nothing and that I, in the ultimate depths of my reality, am Nothing also?" And modern man answers in the only way possible: Whatever is, is right; do your own thing; experience is the only currency left for self-affirmation; self-authentication is sufficient justification for what may result. This response is regarded as legitimate and necessary unless a man wishes for the ultimate experience, suicide (assuming even that that is ultimate). As Bertrand Russell once said, "Only on the foundation of unyielding despair can the soul's habitation be built."

Man oscillates between despair and romanticism, regarding hedonism as a goal and instant happiness as the sole test of what is worthwhile. A tantalizing thirst for stimulation and for continual novelty then leads him ultimately to the negation of his inner motions as a man and to the exhaustion of his creative powers, and he gradually becomes a replica of a human being. Freedom becomes an end in itself—a freedom not to be anything in particular, nor to object to anything in particular, nor even to be responsible for anything in particular. In a nutshell, if God as absolute truth is rejected (and for many modern men that is the case), man is either a victim of determinism or the subjective master of his fate. He experiences the death of hope in the birth of despair, for he sees himself as *no thing*.

It is no wonder that when God is dead man then asks, "Who am I? Do I count?" For "if there is no God, then everything is permitted," and in an open or permissive society, identity crises are bound to be alarmingly frequent. Like the girl in *Jeremy,* we are more and more prone to say, "I don't know who I am. I feel like half a person." *The Sergeant* presents a searing study of the search for identity, affection, even survival. And *The Rain People* is concerned with a woman confused about her identity. In a closed society certain guidelines enabled one at least to survive, but when one acts self-sufficiently, one has somehow to live as though it mattered. To live, or exist, in despair and dread is somehow to be alive but yet aware that one's life has as much significance as a corpse. "I have been a writer but have never been a human being," wrote Hermann Hesse, while R. D. Laing has observed that "there is an 'I' that cannot find a 'me.' " To exist simply as one of the Hollow Men causes despair and creates the need either for stimulation or for something external to oneself to give meaning.

These then are the postulates which currently form the cultural consensus: God is dead; nothing is certain; everything is relative; man is either totally determined or totally free and without bounds of any kind. Not all but many of today's films reflect precisely these existential postulates, postulates that create a cultural consensus and monolithically surround, subsume and suffocate society.

cinema as a laboratory

Twenty, even ten, years ago, the recipe for a successful film was simple and seemed to be secure: Take an exciting or tragic plot, add pinches of romance as required, garnish with a happy ending and sprinkle with stars; project onto a giant screen in either Panavision or Todd AO, possibly in 3D, and you were home and dry. *Ben Hur* or any of John Ford's films (which invariably endorsed the values of home and family, loyalty and courage) come to mind. The effect on the audience was that, in most cases, whatever point the film had was forgotten as soon as the lights went on.

Now many films are made more from an ideology than from an idea; postulates dominate the story. Because of the change in epistemology and in basic postulates, many films are projected not so much in a cinema as in a cinema that is a laboratory, and the viewer, although indeed enjoying and appreciating much of positive achievement and value, may be subjected to a series of experiments carried out on the basis of these postulates. The cinema often becomes a laboratory in the sense that sensitive and intelligent directors not only are feeling their way towards new philosophical and technical expressions within this art form but also are probing for audience reaction and response.

The contemporary cinema has, to some extent, been extruded on the one hand from its original art form and on the other hand from the Hollywood block-buster into the cinema of social communication and social pacesetter, even though a number of films continue rather than create a trend. Nevertheless, directors know what we forget—that by and large the average viewer is sufficiently apathetic and inert that he becomes totally involved in what he is seeing on the screen. One director recently remarked, "You must hit them before they can think," while another observed, "We give the public what it gets." And what the public frequently gets is ambiguity; there is no clear demarcation between good and evil, and there is often ambivalence in verbal statements. One result of this is that the viewer can fantasize as much as he wishes and is under no compulsion to see that he himself has to choose between what is being offered to him. Robert Altman has commented that a "good movie" is "taking the narrative out, taking the story out of it. The audience will sit and see the film and understand the movie's intention without being able to articulate it."

Most of us leave our critical faculties at the box office, and this is not only insulting to all concerned in the production of a film but unwise for at least two reasons. First, the art of film is essentially fluidity and mobility; the greater the fluidity and mobility the more difficult it is for the viewer to arrest, isolate and analyze what he is seeing. Speed is both the factor and the problem; each second, the viewer has twenty-four frames, one-and-a-half feet, of film flick before his eyes and flash upon his mind. In everyday life, the whole vision may be focused with undivided attention upon one object for an indefinite length of time, and this focusing is by choice and is directed by the mind. In the cinema, however, the whole vision is often focused with undivided attention upon a flowing multiplicity of objects; choice is by-passed and the direction is from the camera, that is, from the director. This situation is compounded by darkness, which partly succeeds in eliciting emotional responses which bubble up from the subconscious.

Second, the visual is more potent than the verbal. This is so for one paramount reason: The visual (I am speaking of films augmented by the variety of technical devices) like the verbal touches the conscious level of the mind but, unlike the verbal, penetrates beneath the conscious level to the subconscious and en route affects the emotions and the will. "The film is the greatest teacher," wrote V. I. Pudovkin, "because it teaches not only through the brain but through the whole body." And Bergman talks about using "an apparatus which is constructed to take advantage of a certain human weakness." Bergman has observed also that "film has nothing to do with literature.... The written word is read and assimilated by a conscious act of the will in alliance with the intellect; little by little it affects the imagination and the emotions.... When we experience a film, we consciously prime ourselves for illusion. Putting aside will **33** and intellect, we make way for it in our imagination. The sequence of pictures plays directly on our feelings."

There is no neutrality in film. Both the message of the medium *and* the medium itself touch the conscious level of the mind and elicit a response that is generated by the subconscious. And there is no neutrality in the response. It is interesting to note that when Alex in *A Clockwork Orange* submits to the Ludovico Treatment for a cure for his vicious and violent nature, the material for the conditioning from pleasure to revulsion comes from films "feeding back into his system a surfeit of murder, rape and atrocity." Such conditioning is already being used in some psychiatric practice. We will take up this subject again as we consider certain cinematic danger points.

In an age of relativity—when everything is up for grabs—directors may well give the audience whatever suits the director. And what often suits him is to present his own recognition of the fact and significance of the very relativity which frees him to pursue his own course. That takes both him as artist and us as viewers directly into the area of meaning—more specifically, the meaning of man.

Love Story (1970), Arthur Hiller   *The Last Picture Show* (1971), Peter Bagdanovitch

man's search for meaning: the dimension of sex

3

Man's search for purpose and identity, his deep desire to know that he is not a fleck of foam on the waves of a cosmic ocean, his wish to be assured that he has meaning and import are reflected in many contemporary films. Directors well understand man's cry for individuality in an apparently indifferent universe; often they interpret that cry as inseparable from his fundamental need for love. Variants on Descartes' "I think, therefore I am" are frequently stated on film. In this chapter we examine one: "I copulate, therefore I am," where love gets lost in lust.

i copulate, therefore i am

The Hollywood cloak of love is threadbare, but every now and again new and varied patches are added. In *Bob and Carol, Ted and Alice* this refrain occurs: "What the world needs now is love, sweet love, not just for some but for everyone." This is nearer the mark and distinct from other current statements. In *Last Tango in Paris*, the girl answers the question, "What is love?" by saying, "Love is making love." "Sex, sex is the game; marriage is the penalty," says the aging roué in

Sleuth. Some Call It Loving is a sort of Freudian Mad-Hatter's tea party where the boy and girl act out, as in a play or charade, the steps from courtship onwards. In Bergman's *The Seventh Seal,* Jons says that "Love is another word for lust plus lust plus lust and a damn lot of cheating, falseness, lies and all kinds of other fooling around." The girl in *Love Story* sentimentally observes that "love means never having to say you're sorry." In *Cabaret,* after she has had sex with Fritz, Natalia asks, "Is this love?" and Sally has no answer.

The word *love* is seldom defined. Rather it is given a connotative or emotional flavor which invariably leads to or is associated with sex. We are far away from Robert Burns' "My love is like a red, red rose," and much closer to Hart Crane who aptly expresses the loss of meaning both in word and identity when he writes, "Love, a spent match skating in a urinal."

In many contemporary films the context makes it clear that love equals sex plus nothing. Often some sort of ambivalent and extramarital relationship develops which initially seems to be "real" and valid. This is true of films as widely divergent as *John and Mary* (where the boy and girl appear satisfactorily to have established their respective identities) and others such as *Tea and Sympathy, Summer of '42, The Graduate, The Last Picture Show, The Heart Murmur, Harold and Maude, 40 Carats.* The first six are interesting in that in them a boy or young man goes to bed with an older woman, and it is implied that sex is the Open Sesame for youth's identity. For the woman, the liaison takes place usually because she is herself unsatisfied sexually or is bored or lonely as in *Ryan's Daughter* and *The Last Picture Show.*

The main point I am making is that, in general, sex as delineated on film seems to be regarded as a prime source of personal verification. The moral element, if it occurs at all, comes up in such comments as Maude makes to Harold: "It's best not to be too moral. You teach yourself out of life." And the girl in *Klute* repeats three times, "There's nothing really wrong, is there?" But the girl in *Cabaret* speaks from experience: "Sex always screws up a friendship anyway. . . ." In Nichol's *Carnal Knowledge,* the hero, desperately trying to discover who he is and having staggered through years of sexual disillusionment, hopes that his new woman will lead him to his phallic El Dorado. This film might not unfairly be subtitled: The Quest for the Perfect Orgasm.

Such an honest portrait of a dislocated personality is deeply disturbing because this film appears to argue, as *Last Tango in Paris* forcibly does, for the impossibility of love in a meaningless world. *Klute* also says the same thing: There is no such thing as love; there is only biological appetite, a euphemism for lust. As has been said, the heroines of so many films are whores and if love is an illusion, then who better than whores know how to sustain it?

Cassavétes' existential disclosures in *Husbands* are likewise disturbing. The three men in their self-authenticating carousing never find an answer to their loneliness, emptiness and awareness of inner deterioration; moreover, they are unable to share their common inner experiences in spite of talking a great deal about them. Pinter's *Caretaker* has the same problem. And if Fellini's *La Dolce Vita* says anything, it clarions out that *vita* is by no means all *dolce*.

On a different level are the James Bond films, excitingly trivial and entertaining. Bond is the old-type romantic hero in modern guise, the romantic dream hero of the technological era. Nonetheless, his modern five-fold aims of sex, sadism, snobbery, hedonism and patriotism (or is it nationalism?) somewhat differentiate him from his medieval counterpart. *Live and Let Die*, from *Goldfinger* out of *Thunderball*, disappoints in none of these areas. The usual cavalcade of generously endowed nubile dollies is reduced to the status of a mattress, but there is a faint hint that even James Bond questions the morality of his job as a hired assassin. But the gospel according to Jeremy Bentham continues to be preached: The end justifies the means. In this film there is a full-scale cashing in on the current interest in the occult which slightly overshadows but does not seriously diminish the hero's commitment to a playboy philosophy. You pay your money at the box office and you take your choice: Does Bond reflect our own familiar world of values or has Fleming deliberately overdrawn these values in order to show us how riddled with them we are?

On a different level are films like Pasolini's *The Decameron* and

The Canterbury Tales with their cracking pace and gorgeous pageantry which act as a framework for taking the lid off the cauldron of sex. No doubt it might be argued that these films are bawdy rather than pornographic, and, if one is thinking of Ben Jonson's *Bartholomew Fair* as a comparison, then they should not be labeled pornographic.

Other films that present man's search for meaning and humanness are *The Virgin and the Gypsy* and *Women in Love*. The latter is the female counterpart to *Carnal Knowledge* where two girls are on the brink of sexual maturation and are provided with the opportunity for sexual experience. In *Women in Love,* Gerald asks, "You mean that if there isn't a woman there's nothing?" And Rupert replies, "Pretty well, seeing that there's no God." In *The Virgin and the Gypsy,* the girl's choice is vitiated by the fact that she has to choose between ugly saints and apparently beautiful sinners, but in each of these films D. H. Lawrence's credo is explicit: "My great religion is a belief in the blood, the flesh as being wiser than the intellect. We can go wrong with the mind. But what the blood feels and believes and says is always true." Shades of John Keats! But one wonders whether Lawrence saw the extensions: "Follow the impulses. You're only an animal, so live like one." There are echoes of D. H. Lawrence in *Sunday, Bloody Sunday* as Bob cries, "We're free to do what we want." Like *Last Tango in Paris* and *Cabaret* these films also throw into relief the fact that all too often sex per se throws up barriers between persons.

Neither is any real satisfaction to be found in a bisexual or gay relationship. An older generation may still be adamant against or equivocal about this matter, but among the younger generation it is generally accepted, and among those involved it is of course accepted as normal. Nevertheless, the search for meaning and identity yields no answer in this area either, as *Victim, Detective, Sunday, Bloody Sunday* and *The Boys in the Band* show. The wretched condition of those whom Proust called "sons without a mother" is summed up in one phrase: "Show me a happy homosexual and I'll show you a gay corpse." That these men are depicted as persons rather than problems is a commendable feature of the latter film; Tennessee Williams and Edward Albee have a tendency to show persons first as problems and second as persons. Crowley, who directed *The Boys in the Band,* has the order right but leaves them still trapped in a cage.

pornography: the idolatry of sensuality

No more films need be mentioned in this context because there are few where four bare legs in bed is not thought of as a normal part of the current lifestyle. But I do want to say something about pornography in today's films. Pornography is that aspect in any medium which approves of or encourages obscene or perverted behavior; it elevates sensuality to idolatry. At the opposite extreme, obscenity debases sensuality by profaning or mocking it.

The word *pornography* derives from the Greek word *pórnē* which means "a harlot," and originally the word was used to describe the conduct of harlots. Of late its meaning has been enlarged to cover any form of sexual aberration, and it is difficult sometimes to know whether a film is art or pornography. Borowczyk's *Immoral Tales* has an introduction and five episodes in which the director aims to reveal what he regards as the true nature of man's repressed sexuality. Such alleged didacticism supposedly lifts the film above the pornographic level and poses in addition another question: Does morality put a brake on debauchery or does it encourage it?

Pornography, I am convinced, is as habit forming as any drug and could be said to aim at the abolition of personality. It is as much a spectator sport as wrestling or basketball, and therein lies its condemnation and danger: That which should be private becomes not a peep show but a public spectacle. In addition, many of today's films do not stop at exhibiting copulation; deviant sexual behavior and sado-masochistic perversion are also screened. The effect is to degrade not only sex per se but man himself. One cannot help thinking that an assiduous attempt is being made to upgrade pornography into art and from it produce a philosophy.

Moreover, because of current postulates and semantic mysticism, words like *obscene, perverted, normal, self-expression, moral* are coming to have identical meanings. This is Andy Warhol's position in *Nude Restaurant* and Morrissey's in *Trash* and *Flesh.*[1] In all three, as in Bertolucci's *Last Tango in Paris,* the human body is regarded as an inex-

39

haustible source not of wonder and beauty but of obsession and exploration. The same is true of *The Mother and the Whore* which glimpses the aridity and desolation that accrue from almost endless sexual variety. These films, desperately trying to find a basis for meaning, would have us accept mere sexual activity of any and every kind as the common denominator of all human experience.

Bertolucci's film reaches a point of no return because in a way it is neither less erotic than similar recent films, especially those with an X or XX certificate, nor more erotic than similar future films are likely to be. The erogenous elements which sharply reveal the heart-wounding emptiness of lives lived without meaning are unnecessary because the film does not hinge on pornography as such, despite every Madison Avenue attempt to make us believe it does. From the outset the meaning of the film is clear: Alongside the credits are placed two of Francis Bacon's paintings in both of which man is screaming for meaning and identity, love and humanness. The fierce thrust of this film is that meaningful communication between

40 human beings is impossible in today's absurd world; life is merely a tango (or a "cabaret"), and the steps lead nowhere. Paul says, "I don't have a name," and when the girl is about to tell him hers, he swiftly rejoins, "I don't want to know your name." This is a follow-through from Resnais' *Last Year at Marienbad* where the characters have no names but letters instead (they also have no history, no families, no professions—what is the point if there is no reality?).

In *Last Tango in Paris* there is nothing left in life but self-authentication in masturbation, sodomy, copulation or whatever else is available. As Paul says, "We'll change Chance to Fate." After their liaison, Jeanne and Paul separate and Jeanne returns to be with the young man she is supposed to be marrying. Sitting on the side of a Paris canal, they speak of marriage: "Today advertised marriage is smiling." Still speaking of the subject and the security it offers, they throw a lifebelt into the canal—and it sinks. Jeanne then returns to Paul's apartment and the self-authentication begins again. As Paul says, "We left the apartment. Now we begin again."

One review points out that "in the course of the film [Paul and Jeanne] exchange roles and their entire relationship is like a dialec-

Last Tango in Paris (1973), Bernardo Bertolucci

tic. . . . [Paul] is coming out of a tragic experience which culminates
in the suicide of his unfaithful wife. He has a negative outlook on
marriage and on love, and that is why he wants to know nothing
about Jeanne, why . . . he wants to meet her on the animal level.
But in the end he does not succeed." Both Paul and Jeanne may be
seen in the image of Bacon's painting—burnt out, shriveled replicas
of human beings. On this view of man, the film's conclusion is pre-
dictable and yet again underlines Lindsay Anderson's question:
"Why is it that writers can never write real endings? It's very odd.
Why is it?" In countless novels and films, the conclusion is polarized
between helpless despair and groundless optimism.

"I'm tired of having my mind raped," murmurs Jeanne, a contemporary neophiliac hoping against hope that something new will
be found in sex, that this time sex will remove, not erect, barriers
and that there will be some final experience that will provide meaning to her life. But ultimately, the film choreographs the existentialism of Camus or Sartre with the consequent emptiness and futility of life. Bertolucci, the director, indicated as much in a recent
interview: "*Last Tango* is a film which asks a question: Is it possible
today, in this society, in this system of life for a man or a woman to

have a real relationship? The answer? It is purely personal."

the sociology of sex
With this film in mind, advertised as avant-garde pornography
(outside the private clubs), several things should be considered.
First, perhaps nothing has a greater long-term effect on any person's psychological development and stability, as well as on the psychological condition of society as a whole, than sex. Each person's
psychological development depends for its effectiveness on personal relationships. That development starts with the family, continues with friends and acquaintances and should find fulfillment
in marriage. Within marriage, an important element is a sexual
relationship which both reflects and promotes love between hus-
band and wife. Within this secure relationship, sex is not only enjoyable but enriching.

Second, the social or national implications are far reaching, for
the psychological well-being of society is in proportion to the normality and morality of its members. It can be argued that anything
which moves against the well-being of the family inevitably harms
the fabric of society and the nation. The danger is that when an emphasis is placed on sexual excitement, physical attraction and deviations, sex itself is degraded. Only when physical attraction and
sexual excitement are seen in association with marriage does sex
find its rightful place and, as it were, come into its own. Moreover,
marriage and the concept of the family suffer rather severe setbacks
when sex is isolated from the context of marriage and marital
love.

Third, pornography per se never has anything to say concerning
love. This is the condemnation of the gratuitous pornographic element in *Last Tango in Paris* and in Antonioni's *Blow-Up* with its call
for "love without meaning."[2] In *Blow-Up,* sex is divorced from love
and tenderness and the intention to go on building a secure companionship within marriage; sex is pandered to and exaggerates
the selfishness which is then at its root. The sad fact is that in film
after film bodies writhe and groan, and within and after the sexual
act there is not an atom more love, tenderness and companionship

than there was at the beginning. This is sharply expressed in "The Conclusion," a poem by Steve Turner:

My love
she said
that when all's
considered
we're only machines.

I chained
her to my
bedroom wall
for future use
and she cried.[3]

The attempt to reduce a person to a piece of machinery always fails. When a machine cries, it is no longer a machine.

Fourth, there is a connection between pornography and psycho-sexual disorders. Brady, the murderer of the child in the Moors murder case in Britain, appears to have found pornography an incitement to violence. Arthur Bremmer, the twenty-one-year-old attacker of Governor Wallace in the United States, was described as a solitary individual addicted to sex comics. And a case may also be made for asserting that pornography, in creating an appetite for spiralling sensation, may lead into the further fantasies and disorders of the drug culture.

There is nothing new in pornography; the paintings in Hindu temples, the erotica at Pompeii, the writings of Petronius and Boccaccio are part of this continuity with the past. What is new is the assumption that it will provide meaning and purpose for life and, in short, unite the divided mind, emotions and will. This assumption is based on today's postulates and thought-forms which in turn have produced another phenomenon, namely, the use of sex as an unlimited raw material by commercial interests whose object is to make sex exploitation in its many and varied forms a consumer product.

A hundred years ago it was often considered sinful to enjoy sex; today it is considered sinful not to enjoy it.[4] In fact, one is told one

43

ought to use any means to obtain sexual gratification and utilize any technique to enjoy it when one has got it. Jean Cocteau at the Cannes Film Festival some years ago summed up this attitude when he called the contemporary cinema that "Temple of Sex, with its Goddesses, its Guardians and its Victims." Of course, pornography in a film like *Last Tango in Paris* is mild compared with new hardcore films like *The Devil in Miss Jones, Pink Flamingoes, Deep Throat* and *Deep Throat–Part II*. These make Jezebel seem like a Sunday school teacher and are tipping pornography into non-humanness and irrationality. Beyond the cash returns, it is difficult to see any justification for this kind of film. But there are other kinds of films equally hard to justify.

The Wild Bunch (1969), Sam Peckinpah   *Bonnie and Clyde* (1967), Arthur Penn

man's search for meaning: the dimension of violence

4

The contemporary cinema's attitude toward sex is to some degree matched by its attitude toward violence. This, of course, is no accident; a preoccupation with sex is often an indication of a failure of nerve in the face of despair, in our era a despair induced by not knowing who one is or what life is about.[1] Perhaps to the same extent this is true of violence. Moreover, because of the association between sex and anger, violence or aggression runs neck and neck with sex as a means of trying to establish a viable identity.[2]

if sex, then violence

One of the consequences of being adrift in a world without absolutes is that a person comes to believe that if there is any solution, then it lies in search. Truth will be reached when a problem is pinpointed and explored. There is no *terminus ad quem,* only search. This is part of today's new-romanticism and is evident in the galloping urge to self-destruction that compels those involved, for example, in gambling, drug addiction and alcoholism to deeper involvement and greater risks.[3] Films depicting violence, while reflecting and promoting society's current interest and concern, may also, by diagnosing the disease and demonstrating the dilemma, be suggesting that the solution lies simply in search.

It is difficult to say when this particular trend began. Possibly the first film sequence that showed violence on the screen in the sense in which we are now discussing it was the Odessa steps massacre in Eisenstein's *Battleship Potemkin,* produced in 1925. Nonetheless, *Bonnie and Clyde* and *Butch Cassidy and the Sundance Kid* were certainly both today's watershed and quicksand, soon to be followed by *The Wild Bunch, Wild Angels* and *The Dirty Dozen.* The Vietnam War, student strife, racial conflict and gang warfare may have helped to spark such films as *The Outback, The Cowboys, Dirty Harry, Soldier Blue, Bloody Mama, The Grissom Gang, Play Misty for Me, No One Will Survive, Villain, Joe, Frenzy, Deliverance, Straw Dogs, The Godfather, A Clockwork Orange, Pat Garrett and Billy the Kid, Badlands.*

It is important to distinguish between films *of violence* and films *depicting violence.* None of these mentioned is a film of violence, that is, a film in which violence is displayed for its own sake. Each treats other matters in a responsible manner (as did *Richard the Third, Tamburlaine the Great* and *The Duchess of Malfi* in the Renaissance; there is nothing new in violence either). One may single out *Soldier Blue,* which re-enacts a historical event in one of the U.S. Army campaigns against the Indians; *The Grissom Gang,* which is an adaptation of Nancy Mitford's thriller, *No Orchids for Miss Blandish; Joe* and *Frenzy,* which delineate the development of psychopaths; and *Deliverance,* which is concerned with a contemporary search for the Holy Grail.

There is no reason yet to think that films of violence are being produced, although the same cannot be said for a number of XX sex films in which sex is displayed for its own sake. However, one may well have qualms about a brace of what might be termed pornography of violence films, *Magnum Force* and *Gordon's War.* The former states that justice will be achieved only when the police use on criminals the methods criminals use on the public. The latter asserts that vigilantes alone can clean up a drug scene. It is an oversimplification but it seems to me that pornography is the result of passive resignation, the result of despair at existing in a meaningless world. Violence is a more active response to existing in a meaningless world.

A Clockwork Orange (1972), Stanley Kubrick

These films, reflecting and promoting one of society's problems and re-enacting one or another of an individual's basic instincts (as well as providing release for both sexual and aggressive feelings), are also, upon occasion, visual synopses of existential philosophy. Consider Kubrick's *A Clockwork Orange*. The peculiar title suggests that it is better for a man to possess free will, even if it is the will to do evil, than it is for him to be manipulated into an automatic model of goodness. It is instructive to read what Anthony Burgess wrote about his novel of the same title, which first appeared in 1961 and from which the film was made: "It was intended to be a sort of tract, even a sermon, on the importance of the power of choice. My hero, or anti-hero, is very vicious . . . but his viciousness is not the product of genetic or social conditioning; it is his own thing embarked on in full awareness. He is evil, not merely misguided."

This is a refreshing intimation of a fundamental truth about one part of man's nature: Violence is not in the first place a spontaneous activity; it is an attitude of mind fulfilled in an expression of will. In brief, I am not so much violent by nature as violent by choice. Alex is not naturally inclined toward brutality and Beethoven; he chooses them as he chooses rape and reading. So did some commandants of

German concentration camps who listened to Beethoven in the evening and attended floggings in the morning, thus giving the lie to the belief that there is a valid connection between a person's capacity to respond to art and his general fitness for humane living.[4]

Yet the main thrust of *A Clockwork Orange* is twofold. First, despite Burgess, Kubrick seems to suggest that man might well need B. F. Skinner's social conditioning. After all, there are disturbing signs of society's amoral indecisiveness, clear indications that it has lost its sense of direction. How shall it be held together without some form of social conditioning? But over against this, he strongly asserts man's right to free choice. Second, Kubrick has pushed existentialism to its limits in that Alex authenticates himself to the nth degree. Since personal experience is not describable solely in rational terms, only self-authentication remains: "It is his own thing embarked on in full awareness."

Like many contemporary films, *A Clockwork Orange* moves on several levels simultaneously—social, political, moral, theological—
while still retaining the continuity of the story. It is not a film of violence or of the moral implications of violence; in its scenes of violence it is no more offensive, though more subtle, than any barroom brawl in a western. Essentially, the film concerns itself with asserting the fact of free choice and the need to preserve it against conditioning. When Alex agrees to submit to the Ludovico Treatment, the prison Chaplain says that the Governor has grave doubts about it. But Alex insists he does not care about the dangers; he just wants to be good. To this the Chaplain replies, "The question is not whether or not this technique really makes a man good. Goodness comes from within. Goodness is chosen. When a man cannot choose he ceases to be a man." There is another significant exchange between the Chaplain and the Minister of the Interior on the same subject:

> *Chaplain:* Choice? The boy has not a real choice, has he? Self-interest, the fear of physical pain drove him to that grotesque act of self-abasement. The insincerity was clear to be seen. He ceases to be a wrongdoer. He ceases also to be a creature capable of moral choice.

Minister: Padre, these are subtleties. We are not concerned with motives, with the higher ethics. We are concerned only with cutting down crime.... The point is that it [the treatment] works.[5]

The issue of choice rises again in Peckinpah's *Straw Dogs,* which shows what happens to a man who fails to make certain choices, knowing full well that they should be made. Passing the point of no return and aided by his wife's equivocal loyalty, David is forced into violence. It is the only choice left. At the same time, it is not easy to avoid the impression that *Straw Dogs* is stating that sex and violence are basic to what man intrinsically is and that these constitute the perimeter of man's existence. As has been said, the way to womanhood leads through violation; there is really no such thing as rape. By the same token, a man out of touch with his primal instincts is not yet real. Indeed, with reference to violence and the public, Peckinpah admitted in an interview that he intended "to rub their noses in it." But what he has succeeded in doing is to push nihilism to its furthest limits yet.

51

involving the viewer in violence

Films of sex and violence might in the future become justified on the grounds that they allegedly provide insights into the nature of man. We close one eye if we "write off" these films as concerned solely with sex and violence; we close the other eye if we pretend that they are not designed to make an impact on us and get us involved.

An obvious way to involve the viewer, and directors know how to make the most of it, is to create within us a feeling of pity or sympathy for the hero or villain. This of course in not new; Shakespeare does it for Richard III and Webster for de Bosola in *The Duchess of Malfi.* The villain is frequently engaging and charming. In Tuchner's *Villain* the lead character demonstrates a natural love and intense care for his mother. Love and loyalty within the family and hatred and viciousness outside of it form the warp and woof of *The Godfather, Bonnie and Clyde* and *Butch Cassidy and the Sundance Kid.* Such films play ping-pong with our emotions, for we are attracted and repulsed at the same time; it is like traffic lights flashing alternately red and green. Then too, it is sometimes impossible to differentiate between the "good guys" and the "bad guys." In *The Sting*, for example, both sides are involved in the same racket and use the same methods. *Foxy Brown* takes the same line. Not only are many of today's film heroes equivocal in their integrity but many of the "bad" are appealing in their "humanness."

Is it going too far to suggest that if we get too involved, then to some extent we become accessories after the fact, aiding the sex and abetting the violence? Perhaps more important, it is now realized that a banquet of sex and violence is by no means necessarily cathartic. It does not always purge nor satisfy nor eliminate the desire for more, nor by a process of attrition does it produce a revolting repugnance. Some evidence suggests that a *desire* may speedily become a *need* which, like drug addiction, escalates a need for more. The subconscious is dangerously stirred and constructive thinking is held in abeyance. Anger may rise within and partly be simulated, and frustration may lacerate. The youths in New York, who after seeing *A Clockwork Orange* went out to perform what they had seen on the screen, support this argument.

On the other hand, British doctors who examined the reactions of a number of medical colleagues to *A Clockwork Orange* and *Soldier Blue* reported that, while excitement was observed, revulsion was the major reaction. Biochemical tests were made prior and subsequent to the films, and heartbeats were monitored during the performance. During the violent episodes, heartbeats slowed down in the same irregular fashion that occurs when passersby witness a serious road accident, and this slowing down of the heartbeat may cause a person to faint when the revulsion becomes too great. Exploiting such reactions, *The Laughing Policeman* explores current attitudes to violence almost, it seems, with an intention not to create revulsion but to induce amnesia. Certainly the most human response to violence in film is not neutral.

O Lucky Man! proceeds on social, moral, psychological, mythical and comic levels. Anderson, the director, once wrote, "The artist must always aim beyond the limits of tolerance. His duty is to be a monster." As a piercing examination of contemporary society, it is moral in the sense that it appeals to reason. The psychological level of the film lies in its understanding (as in *If*) of the hypocrisies that stifle individuality and creativity. It is mythical in that the hero is a sort of pilgrim who progresses from one experience to another without ever reaching his goal. The comedy is rapid and unexpected, and it acts as a buffer against what Anderson calls "strong humanist statements." The film is little short of a documentary on a society that is loose from its moorings; it is shot through with satire and with savage songs that, like the technical devices, both comment on and amplify the film's philosophical statement. One song emphasizes the absurdity of the existentialist world: "So smile while you're making it, laugh while you're taking it, even though you're faking it, nobody's gonna know." When discussing the film with the scriptwriter, Anderson is reputed to have said, "What can anyone be after all in a world where nothing spiritual matters any more? What's he after? . . . Why is it that writers can never write real endings? It's very odd. Why is it?" One of the songs emphasizes the emptiness: "If you've found the reason to live and not die, you are a lucky man." **53**

Many of the cast double up their roles, but this common link of man with man is not enough to prevent breakdown because, as one character says, "If you want something, just take it." The doubling up likewise emphasizes the motif of chance that is at the core of the film: No one knows who he is; no one has any say in who he is. The ebullient optimism of the final scene in which all the characters meet for a party climaxes, Camus-like, in a prison, the guests singing, "And it's around and round and round and round and round we go, and it's around the world in circles turning, So it's on and on and on and it's on and on, round the world in circles turning." The final line of the script reads, "As the song and the film end, we iris in through the tumult of people and balloons on to Mick, still dancing, still reaching out. . . ." Haven't we read something like that before? Even so, despite the existentialism, the film seeks to affirm rather than deny life.

i kill, therefore i am

"No area must be barred to it," says Astruc. "Passions are very precisely its province." Directors, accepting this view, are exploring other avenues in their search for meaning and identity in an apparently absurd if not hostile world. Still within the area of violence, it would seem that *Bonnie and Clyde* (based on true events between 1931 and 1934), *Butch Cassidy and the Sundance Kid*, *Thomasine and Bushrod* and the conclusion of *Easy Rider* assert that killing is fun if not funny. Their winsomeness blended with sly humor tends to anesthetize the viewer against the appalling nature of their activities. Not only is hedonism seen to be an important goal, but subjectivism implies that experience is the only currency left for self-affirmation. The practical consequences of a belief are made the sole test of truth: The real man is a man who has killed a man. In André Malraux's novel *La Condition Humaine* the terrorist Chen utters one of the most excoriating statements of our time: "A man who has never killed is a virgin." That is to say, the act or fact of killing is an act or fact of knowing. *Neco ergo sum:* I kill, therefore I am. And this does not mean that I kill retributively, in war or for a cause, but that I kill **54** arbitrarily.

Killing for killing's sake may be seen in *Badlands,* based on the true story of Charlie Starkweather who in 1958 went on a killing spree similar to that described in *In Cold Blood.* An early scrap of dialogue sets the scene: "I'll give you a dollar if you eat that collie." Kit replies, "I wouldn't do it for a dollar and besides, he's not a collie." From the outset, then, murder is accepted as something to joke about. As Rap Brown said, "Violence is as American as apple pie." Moreover, the characters in the film have no roots, no responsibilities except to themselves. Kit is engaged in the pursuit of happiness, and, as one reviewer says, "If that happiness depends on killing a few people, why then, they will just have to be killed—the same way that the Indians who roamed these prairies were killed, just to get them out of the way." It would seem that many characters in today's films resort to violence not so much because they are inherently sadistic as that they have no other way of dealing with one another. All too often it is the easiest way to continue and conclude the story; it is a surrender, not a solution.

Making the most of viewers' fantasies, directors may find that truth is stranger than fiction because there is a harvest waiting to be cut. *Badlands* and *Bonnie and Clyde* are only the first fruits; consider the cinematic possibilities in such characters as Dutch Schultz, "Baby Face" Nelson, Jack the Ripper, "Pretty Boy" Floyd, Lizzie Borden, John Dillinger, "The Scottsboro Boys," and Leopold and Loeb.

Violence may be not just as American as apple pie but as human as the common cold. If that is all we learn from current films depicting violence, we will be richer for it. But if we are to find a prescription for this wretched condition of man, we will have to look elsewhere than to the films we have been considering. They are rather long on diagnosis, rather short on cure.

Midnight Cowboy (1969), John Schlesinger   *The Sting* (1973), George Roy Hill

man's search for meaning: tripping, working, playing

5

It appears necessary for some to resort to sex and violence as sources for discovering meaning to life. These topics have been considered at length because they play such a large role in contemporary film and contemporary life. But there are other ways to maintain that a human being has worth and perhaps even dignity.

i trip, therefore i am
In the context of the quest for reality and meaning, drug addiction or dependence has not gone unnoticed. *Chappaqua,* a poorly constructed film, is yet a stark statement about the hallucinatory world of drug addiction and alcoholism. *Gordon's War* and *Hit* are apt portrayals, though they appear to advocate vehement vigilante tactics to deal with the drug problem, thus seemingly recommending the establishment of an elite outside the law, like that in *Magnum Force,* and in due course exposing the participants themselves to attack. In this connection, the hero of *Joe,* a blue-collar worker incensed by the dissipated life of the drug world, also takes the law into his own hands in a particularly horrifying way. The drug sequences framed

in *More* and *Panic in Needle Park* and to some extent in *Alice's Restaurant* and *Candy* capture the poignant misery of those moving on what they thought would be an escalator to infinity but which has become in fact a slide into hell.

Still, while directors have taken the drug world as a theme, few, if any, have found that the psychedelic scene provides a meaningful backdrop to human existence.

i work, therefore i am

Work, too, is often seen as something by which to establish identity. In this area, *Medium Cool*, *The Arrangement* and *The Graduate* are cases in point. The first typifies the merciless monomania of a man who makes a career his only reference point and ultimate object. *Citizen Kane* has the same overtones. In order to achieve his end, Kane makes himself an absolute monarch in commerce and, as a result, like Cain, "kills" his brother and the ideals he once held. In *The Graduate*, Benjamin's father evinces a similar commercial concern when **58** he asks his son, "But what are you going to *do*, Benjamin?"

Serpico is interesting in this connection, too. Serpico resolutely fights the monolithic corruption at both higher and lower levels among those with whom he works in the police force. As a result, he is hated, feared and isolated, and his courageous struggle over eleven years ends in only partial success. But the reason for his stand is never given. He establishes an identity that we can certainly admire but probably not respect. *The Super Cops* is another real-life story of two police officers who resolutely and almost single-handedly clean up a thug-infested neighborhood.

With more perception, *The Damned* and *The Conformist* reveal the destruction of the inner man when commitment to the tyrannous claims of a career becomes absolute. Perhaps the clearest exposure of this is Antonioni's *Red Desert* where the depersonalization of man in a technological society is starkly silhouetted.

These films among others disclose the fragmenting of the organic unity of personality into something less than human, something brutal and brutalizing, the near transformation of man into a piece of machinery. This depersonalization appears greatest in the city where men and women tend to lose their awareness of who they intrinsically are as the injection of the impersonal attitudes and forces of society penetrate, blur and sometimes dissolve their organic unity.

Midnight Cowboy searingly recalls the stabbing awareness of this and suggests that Ratso and Joe Buck, caught in the mechanistic maelstrom, are the victims of chemical determinism. A film reminiscent in some respects of *Midnight Cowboy* is *Scarecrow,* which basically is concerned with the pursuit of the American Dream but also lovingly portrays the developing relationship between two losers and innocents abroad.

Who or what is Man? is very much the concern of today's directors and playwrights as again and again they focus unerringly and honestly on aspects of man's nature and dilemma. Eventually, however, they come round to the view of H. G. Wells: "Man has only naked existence; there is no way out or round or through." Man is The Naked Ape, Beyond Freedom and Dignity, and there is little uniqueness or importance to distinguish him from anything else in the universe, natural or mechanical.

It follows, then, that man has no survival value. Bertrand Russell once observed, "When I die I shall rot and that will be the end of me." And A. J. Ayer has said, "I don't expect to survive my death in any sense at all." *They Shoot Horses, Don't They?* is a brilliant, frightening commentary on both depersonalization and nonsurvival, displaying not only the endless dilemmas of man in the symbolism of the continuous race but also the non-significance of man. It is a desperately sad echo of Bertrand Russell and A. J. Ayer.

i play, therefore i am

Man sees work in different ways: as a means of establishing his identity; as an anodyne; as a means of subsisting; as a means of increasing his affluence; as a means of rising socially; as an interruption of his leisure; and occasionally as a creative activity bringing personal fulfillment. But man invariably sees play as a necessity and a right to which he is continually entitled. Directors, however, tend to manipulate and distort man's legitimate pursuit of pleasure.

American Graffiti, a nostalgic excursion into the early 60s, throbs with ennui and the need to try to assuage boredom. So, night after night, the kids cruise through the town in a car, smart clothes, accompanied by or looking for any girl. "What's new?" is the nightly, brittle hope. From another angle, *Bonnie and Clyde* and *Butch Cassidy and the Sundance Kid* see life as a game and killing as one of the moves in that game. Bonnie and Clyde, for example, frequently take photographs of each other because for them life is a picnic. In *Thieves Like Us,* where the emphasis is on the helplessness and emptiness confronting the robbers as they blindly move in the existential fog swirling around them, the play is prolonged in the hope that they will win. *The Sting,* a noteworthy piece of cinematic craftsmanship, sees life as a game in which there are no rules and no values. Roles have to be played rather than goals achieved, and he who shows quick-witted indifference will survive. Man simply manufactures a game plan and calls it life. This film, like a number we are considering, is splendid entertainment.

Duffy and *The Thomas Crown Affair* are films that suggest it is fun to "beat the system." Society is to be disrupted not for gain or by violence but for sheer sport. Even though it may be puerile, there is here at least some positive approach! These two films do not have the appealing anti-heroic element which is present in *The Sting,* where the alleged "good guys" con the "bad guys"—and con us, the audience!

As mentioned earlier, formerly vice had to be punished and virtue rewarded. But because of today's postulates and thought-forms, values have changed. The "domestic virtues," as typified in the monumental films of John Ford, seem to have made an uneasy alliance with some cops and most robbers and anti-heroes. In this context, *The Godfather* and *Villain* have already been mentioned.

Not so long ago, despite some unhappiness and unsuitability, the domestic virtues seemed to be secure within marriage. For many, "I marry, therefore I am" was not only a hope but a fact. Today many cracks are appearing in the structure of marriage and are reflected on film. *Family Life* does nothing to repair this but rather creates greater destruction in that the contestants behave more like cannibals than human beings, while *Till Death Do Us Part* and *Plaza Suite* humorously endeavor to plaster over the cracks. *Divorce American Style* anticipates in one scene a possible future development—a family based on relationships between divorced and remarried couples. An explosive film on the subject of marriage is *Alpha Beta,* an acetylene statement that sees marriage as "one of the few remaining forms of ritual slaughter." *The Way We Were* again underlines the lack of understanding of the many factors that go toward a happy marriage, not the least that, like a daily task, it has to be worked at. The film also illuminates the era of the 40s and 50s.

It is worth remarking that the "I am heroic, therefore I am" mentality epitomized in such films as *Ben Hur, Drums along the Mohawk, Spartacus, The Guns of Navarone* and *The Bridge over the River Kwai* seems to have disappeared without trace. No longer does the hero stride like a Colossus into, through and out of the film. Rather, he is replaced by an anti-hero, who limps his way through as in *O Lucky Man!* The anti-hero acts out on film what is all too often true in life. With the loss of a high view of Man, man has little dignity, value or worth; his highest honesty is only to his emotions. Moreover, he may actually "get away with it" as happens in *The Getaway* and in *Charley Varrick.* In the latter, the rope of confusion is tied with the knot of misunderstanding because it is Walter Matthau, an avuncular teddy bear, who "gets away with it."

Another former heroic type, the psychiatrist, is also under a cloud. At one time in films he had superseded the pastor—always good for a laugh but now the object of ironic ridicule—and from *Spellbound* (made in 1945) to the mid-60s, the psychiatrist figured as a wise and sympathetic miracle worker. But by the end of the 60s even he had lost his credibility. The psychoanalyst in *What's New, Pussycat?* is certainly more crazy than his patients, and *Take the Money and Run* has in one scene a shrewd take-off on the psychiatrist. Perhaps, as is the custom in fashions, the wheel will come full circle again. In fact, *The Exorcist* points in that direction.

The Seventh Seal (1957), Ingmar Bergman   *Five Easy Pieces* (1970), Robert Rafelson

man's search for meaning: the dimension of religion

While many directors and film makers seek in the twin themes of sex and violence an answer to man's deepest longings for meaning and significance, some have recognized that the answer, whatever it turns out to be, will involve the religious dimension. A few, such as Bergman, have been both explicit and profound in their treatment. But others touch it more tangentially. Some even try to make a religion out of hopes and dreams, having a misty hope that in the future their search will terminate in satisfaction.

neo-romanticism and the happy corpse

Attempts to establish such a faith in the future are nothing more than a rebirth of romanticism. Neo-romanticism is "philosophically a crusade to glorify man's existence; psychologically . . . the desire to make intolerable life tolerable." Truffaut's *Jules et Jim* depicts the attempt to escape into an illusory world, where it is Catherine herself who effects the transition from one to the other insofar as she seems to be alternately "an irresponsible tyrant or a liberating muse."

Widerberg's *Elvira Madigan* is a superb exposé of a view of life that has no basis in reality; the illusive images of security that are provided are the product of romanticism. The fantasy spiral reaches its apotheosis in this beautifully handled film and endorses Tolstoy's dictum: "Romanticism comes from the fear of looking straight into the eyes of Truth."

Antonioni's *Zabriski Point* proceeds on several levels, but one may see the optimistic answer around the corner in the final frame where Daria drives towards a roseate sunset. Enjoyable as it is, *The Sound of Music* insists, despite the Nazis, that man really lives in a friendly world. *West Side Story* ends with a hopeful hymn to togetherness: "We'll find a new way of forgiving, somewhere." The end of Rafelson's *Five Easy Pieces* shows the hero, Bob, having divested himself of his few remaining possessions in order to hang free, hitching a lift on a truck which then drives him in the same direction from which he had come. One is reminded of the conclusion to *Luther* where Luther, deeply doubting whether all has been for the best, says, "Let's just hope so." Fitzgerald's novel *The Great Gatsby* concludes with these words: "Gatsby believed in the green light, the orgiastic future that year by year recedes before us. It eluded us then, but that's no matter—tomorrow we will run faster, stretch out our arms farther. . . . And one fine morning—so we beat on, boats against the current, borne back ceaselessly into the past." The conclusion of William Golding's novel *The Pyramid* is in the same vein; Oliver, says the narrator, got into his car and "moved away . . . at last on to the motor road. I concentrated resolutely on my driving." How right Renan was when he wrote, "We are living on the perfume of an empty vase."

Guillaume Apollinaire, the champion successively of Cubism, Dadaism and Surrealism, once cried, "We have set out as pilgrims whose destination is perdition . . . across streets, across countries and across reason itself." And that is an agonizing echo of Baudelaire: "Only when we drink poison are we well. We want—this fire so burns our brain tissue—to drown in the abyss, heaven or hell. Who cares? Through the unknown we'll find the new." Here is the quintessence of romanticism: Complete trust is placed in the validity of

Cabaret (1972), Bob Fosse

a unique, personal insight in which the primacy of subjective vision is total. Ultimately, however, this leads to inner destruction and, as in *Elvira Madigan*, to the Death Wish. The same is true of *The Music Lovers,* where romanticism and tragedy go hand in hand.

An ancillary to romanticism is nostalgia as exhibited in *Paper Moon, The Last Picture Show* and *Cabaret.* This sour side of the American Dream comes to light in other films also, such as *Janice. Rebel without a Cause,* like *The Last Picture Show,* is concerned with youthful maladjustment and the high cost and possibly questionable worth of integration into contemporary society. *The Last Picture Show* vividly discloses more than the feeling of an era that is gone or the illusion of innocence that is past or of kids growing up in a town running down. It is not so much that we are asked to accept this portrait of a sterile community but rather that we are to become stonily resigned to it.

Cabaret, a film concentrating on a sado-masochistic nightclub typical of pre-Hitlerite Germany, is set in Berlin in 1931. With no little panache, it reveals the games people play to cover their lack of identity and the hedonistic façade of the cabaret covering the fears of society. But it is also an amalgam of nostalgia and romanticism.

Nonetheless, Sally drops her mask once to reveal her insecurity and, at the back of that, her need to be loved. The cabaret Master of Ceremonies ironically sings, "Life is a cabaret, come to the cabaret. . . . Here life is beautiful, we have no troubles here." Such is the background to a film that explores also the slavery that involves women in acting out fantasies that have lost whatever social value they may once have had. In this film as in *Dyn Amo* and many others, woman is seen as a programmed seductress offering instant indulgence and gratification.

If *The Damned* discloses the corruption within the Nazi party, then *Cabaret* reveals the sleazy, urbane decadence within society at large. With its symbolism of the dance *Cabaret* parallels *They Shoot Horses, Don't They?* with its symbolism of the race. Toward the end of *Cabaret*, Sally sings about the death of a prostitute: "From the cradle to the tomb, it's not a long stay. . . . She was the happiest corpse I have ever seen. . . ." This is a fitting end to a film that with such élan delineates the vacuum of unfulfilled lives. It is a powerful comment on

the fact that all too often the romantic life is the tragic life and the tragic life is the romantic life. *The Great Gatsby* well illustrates this. Nick says to Gatsby, "You can't repeat the past," and Gatsby rejoins, "You can't repeat the past? Of *course* you can!" And speaking of Gatsby after his death, Nick comments that "he had a romantic readiness I have never seen in any other person."

Electra Glide in Blue and *American Graffiti* spell a scenario which maintains that there is nothing beyond man's five senses. In the latter Kurt says to his former girl friend, "Where are you going?" and she replies, "Nowhere." Kurt then asks, "Can I come along too?" A similar question is asked in *The Sting:* "Where are you going?" "I don't know. It depends on what train I get on."

If man is to find meaning, he will not find it in mystical humanism or in nostalgia. It will have to come from something much more substantial. A hint of this seeps through from *Alice's Restaurant*. Toward the end, after the hippies have drifted away, Ray asks Alice, "What went wrong? We tried to build something beautiful here." This cry of bewilderment and pathos is one of the most eloquent in contemporary cinema and finds a parallel in Losey's *Figures in a*

Landscape, where one deserter on the run says to his comrade as their inner degeneracy and outward deterioration become aggravated as the net closes in, "What *have* we done to ourselves?" The heroine in Schatzberg's *Puzzle of a Downfall Child* muses, "I do long for grace, to know grace." In *Wild Strawberries* Isak asks, "Is there no grace?" And Alman replies, "Don't ask me. I don't know anything about such things." A line from Agnes' diary in *Cries and Whispers* reads somewhat more positively: ". . . human contact, friendship, solidarity. I think this is what is called grace." From a believer's point of view, Bresson's *The Diary of a Country Priest* examines what is meant by grace. In Lumet's heart-rending *The Pawnbroker,* the pawnbroker cries, "All I ask and want is peace and quiet within myself." One is reminded of C. G. Jung, who sadly observed, "Life is, or has, meaning and meaninglessness. I cherish the anxious hope that meaning will preponderate and win the battle." Such groundless optimism is part of today's neo-romanticism.

The writer Georges Simenon, who lives in a luxurious villa above Lausanne in Switzerland, has noted, "I have only one ambition left: to be completely at peace with myself. I doubt if I shall ever manage it. I do not think it is possible for anyone. . . . I write because if I did not I should die." He is the author of over 190 books. Speaking of his villa, he comments, "I have tried to build a kind of perfection here but I confess I have not achieved it." In *The Entertainer,* Archie Rice says, "I'm dead behind these eyes," and one is also reminded of Pete Townsend's lines from "The Seeker": "I'm happy when life's good and when it's bad, I cry; I've got values but I don't know how or why." Recently Art Garfunkel commented, "The other day I was thinking 'how much peace have I had?'—that's being truly peaceful from head to toe—and it came to about an hour and a half's worth. . . . I must strive to make some more comfort in my soul." Rod Steiger speaks for all those undergoing agony in the search for meaning: "I would like to leave behind the memory that man is good and that I know what I am. But I *don't* know who I am and what it's all about."

christianity not the answer

If it is obvious that these longings can be satisfied only in a religious context, it is also obvious that film makers do not look to Christianity to provide that context. *M.A.S.H.* and *Catch 22* make humorous sallies at Christianity, the former burlesqueing the Last Supper, the latter parodying the clergy. A parallel to *M.A.S.H.* is Bunuel's *Viridiana* where, during a drunken orgy, rogues and vagabonds are sprawled at a long table in a travesty of da Vinci's picture of the Last Supper.

With *Easy Rider* exposing some of the hypocritical formalities of religion and *Midnight Cowboy* etching one of the bizarre deviations in the cults, more nails are driven into Christianity's coffin. *If* has a field day with the two-facedness of the English Public School Chaplain and the irony involved in the appeal to "fight the good fight." Strick's *Janice* gives us cameos of America, among them a radio commercial advertising a model of Jesus Christ with "genuine, simulated blood" gushing out of him and an illustrated Bible for those who cannot read! *The Virgin and the Gypsy* manifests the all too frequent marriage between orthodox belief and ugly living. Even the brief intimation concerning the monolith in *2001: A Space Odyssey* is instructive: "It has remained completely inert, its origin and purposes still a total mystery." Kubrick said that "the God concept" is at the heart of the film. But it has to be remembered that Kubrick interprets religious experience as transcendent intelligence rather than as the worship of the infinite-personal God.

Religious belief today is stunningly expressed in *La Dolce Vita,* which opens with a scene in which a huge statue of Christ with open arms is being carried across Rome swinging helplessly from a helicopter. *Don't Look Now* contains both verbal and visual shafts about superstition and faith and the worldliness of religion. *Five Easy Pieces* has a deeply felt symbolical scene between the estranged father and son, but it is a monologue rather than a meeting, as the father is paralyzed and speechless. This scene is the more pathetic because it is the only occasion when the son is able to communicate with his father or any other person. In *Cool Hand Luke*, Luke accepts a wager that he cannot eat fifty eggs. Within an hour he has done so and is seen lying on a table in the bunkhouse, arms outstretched and feet crossed. One of his mates, as he looks at him, observes, "Not even *he* could eat fifty eggs."

The Ruling Class is a blitzkrieg on all established verities; it smashes nearly everyone and everything in sight. Artistically, it is superb, being short on neither dazzle nor razzle. It concerns a paranoiac who thinks he is God. He sadly observes, "I stand outside myself watching myself watching myself." And when he is asked, "How do you know you are God?" he triumphantly retorts, "When I pray to Him, I find I'm talking to myself." This and much more in the film makes mincemeat of Christianity as popularly understood. *In the Name of the Father* is social satire and allegory at the expense of Christianity. During a college chapel service a statue comes alive and embraces a masturbating student, while from inside a coffin a priest obsessed with death lectures a student.

In *The Magic Christian,* when the passengers on board the ship of that name look out of the portholes sometime after sailing, they find that they are back at the port from which they departed. The ship had never left. *Paper Moon* is about a Bible-selling hustler, one Moses Prey, who is a con-man. *Marjoe* is a satirical commentary on the gullibility of certain tent revival meetings and the shameless gimmickry of some evangelists and preachers. In one way it is an honest statement, but it is also crude. Marjoe is intermittently filmed sitting around with his trendy friends carving up the poor suckers over whose eyes he has pulled the wool.

Jesus Christ Superstar, despite its title as a Rock Opera and the skillful variety and rich color of its music, adds to the mockery and confusion, insofar as it is, as one reviewer says, "the celebration of image at the expense of substance, a special ingredient of Romanticism, the apotheosis of gimmickry masquerading as the expansion of consciousness." Like Bernstein's *Mass, Jesus Christ Superstar* is a celebration of man's divinity and God's humanity. Under the heading "Epistle from the Philistines," a review in *Time* begins, "Hey, Jesus, what's happening, baby?" and ends, *"Superstar* is really flip city. We're all totally freaked. Hare Krishna." Likewise *Godspell's* attempt to be realistic and contemporary may militate against its being taken seriously, not to speak of its equivocal conclusion.

According to the reported view of the executive board of the Danish Film Institute, the film provisionally entitled *The Love Life of*

Jesus Christ has been described as pornographic, obscene and blasphemous and full of love, vibrancy, warmth and humanity, a judgment that appears to provide for all eventualities except a flop.

Films like *The Greatest Story Ever Told, King of Kings, The Ten Commandments, The Gospel according to Saint Matthew* and *Bible* probably do little direct harm but may well cause indirect harm and, in any event, can hardly be regarded as illuminating statements of Christian belief. All these films and similar attacks on and indictments of Christianity in particular have one thing in common: There is little if any understanding of what biblical Christianity is. The greatest responsibility for this must be laid at the Christian's door. The frequent unreality of a Christian's life and worship; his ignorance of what biblical Christianity is; his timidity in the face of social and political injustice; his inadequacy in the face of intellectual attack; his naiveté concerning the nature of contemporary thought-forms and lifestyles; his lack of unconditional and steady love; and his failure to practice the truth in love—all these severely militate against Christianity's being taken seriously.

In the light of biblical doctrines and ethics, what is the non-Christian to think of the balderdash of the late-nineteenth-century sects and the bunkum of the proliferating twentieth-century cults? Or racist churches? Or churches where those with a gay problem are asked to leave? Or practicing gay churches? Or churches and tent meetings where the latest child preacher-cum-healer or gospel mountebank is generating a great deal of heat and scarcely any light? Or churches which applaud *Jesus Christ Superstar*? Moreover, what is to be made of liberal theology whose workmen have been sawing off the branches of the tree on which they are sitting and then grafting them onto twentieth-century secular thought-forms? Christians themselves are largely to blame for their low image in contemporary films. The films simply "tell it like it is."

Still, two recent films do try to be slightly positive about Christianity. *The Poseidon Adventure* uses a morality play approach but turns out to be both existential in its thinking and man-centered in its positive affirmation, for Preach's sermon endorses the God-is-dead theology. And Zeffirelli's *Brother Son, Sister Moon* has been variously described as "picturesque but superficial," "too much reverential deference to the hippie lifestyle," "an art gallery master-piece of suffocating chicness." One is not inclined overmuch to dis-agree with these strictures, but at least Zeffirelli is aware of the reality of the unseen world and honest in his references to it.

bergman: the silence of god

Instead of attacking Christianity, Ingmar Bergman relentlessly in-quires whether it is valid and concludes that it is not. His films, artistic and articulate triumphs, are an autobiographical library reflecting the fear of and isolation from his father, a Swedish pastor; his developing introspection as a boy which resulted in his making a cinematograph and the new world that this opened to him; and the influence of his literary mentors, Dostoevsky and Strindberg. At the age of nineteen he lost his faith and, soon after, his first love and then a close friend.

It is no accident that his films are, with rare exceptions, made in black and white, for he knows that the issue for man is a stark *either-or:* Either God is there and has spoken, or God is not there and has not spoken. **71**

For Bergman, God is dead; therefore, he is silent. That is, God never was and man is on his own. But this brings Nausea and a Sick-ness unto Death because there is something in man which craves for meaning, purpose and humanness. The resulting despair, as Berg-man sees it, leads to self-authentication in a continual reconnais-sance for reality.

In Bergman's work, some thirty-three films over a period of twenty-five years, two recurring themes are dominant: the search for true revelation and the search for satisfying relationships. Both themes require a moral approach. Bergman stated in an interview, "The only thing we can and should deal with in dramatic form are the ethical subjects. . . . Our whole existence is built up around this concept that there are things we may do and other things we may not do, and it is these complications which we continually come in con-tact with during our entire life."

As far as possible, Bergman relates man to his natural environment with an ambivalent conception of nature as a force to be reckoned with. In *The Seventh Seal,* which is like a medieval morality play, Bergman considers the relation of man with God through the eyes of a knight and his squire returning through a plague-swept countryside to his castle and his final brush with Death. Speaking of faith, the knight remarks that it is "a torment. . . . It is like having someone who is out there in the darkness but never appears, no matter how loudly you call." In an extract from one scene the knight and Death converse:

Knight: Do you hear me?

Death: Yes, I hear you.

Knight: I want knowledge, not faith, not supposition but knowledge. I want God to stretch out His hand toward me, reveal Himself and speak to me.

Death: But He remains silent.

Knight: I call out to Him in the dark but no one seems to be there.

Death: Perhaps no one is there.

Knight: Then life is an outrageous horror. No one can live in the face of death knowing that all is nothingness.[1]

The knight's agony finds an echo in Wittgenstein's words: "Whereof one cannot speak, thereof one must be silent." Bertrand Russell remarked, "We stand on the shore of an ocean, crying to the night and the emptiness. Sometimes a voice answers out of the darkness but it is the voice of one drowning and in a moment the silence returns." Likewise, Jons says, "Emptiness . . . we are helpless," but the knight cries, "God, who are somewhere, who *must* be somewhere." The film ends with the knight apparently giving his life for others "in faith." But if this noble action is his intention, we have, in view of Bergman's deep questioning, to ask what is meant by "faith."

The trilogy of *Through a Glass Darkly, Winter Light* and *The Silence* asks the same question: Does God exist? In the first, the schizophrenic Karen sees God as a spider on a wall. Does this mean that God is merely a chimera of a diseased mind? Tomas, the pastor in *Winter Light*, says, "Every time I confronted God with the reality I saw, He became ugly, revolting, a spider-god, a monster. That's why

Winter Light (1963), Ingmar Bergman

I hid Him away from the light, from life. . . ." Tomas gazes up at the
wooden crucifix in the deserted church and sobs, "My God, my God,
why have you abandoned me?" Then follows this scene description
in the script: "God's silence, Christ's twisted face, the blood on the
brow and the hands, the soundless shriek behind the barred teeth."
Tomas eventually whispers, "No, God does not exist any more." For
Bergman as for Tomas, there is only the "spider-god," the "lie-god,"
the "echo-god."

In *The Silence,* one main consequence of God's death is examined:
Humanness and personal relationships cease to have any real meaning. It is said of Bergman that he once stood in a church in front of a
painting of Christ and asked him to speak to him. Christ did not;
"there was only silence." Some years ago Beckett said, "Where I am,
I don't know. I'll never know. In the silence you don't know; you
must go on. I can't go on. I'll go on." And Jean-Paul Sartre has commented, "That God is silent, that I cannot deny. That everything
within me cries out for God, that I cannot forget."

Persona endeavors to penetrate beyond the surface of what seems
to a hoped-for reality behind what is. The actress refuses to speak.
The film itself is seen being burnt through by the projection light as

the director throws it on the screen for himself. He too will decline to speak. And that refusal, as the film shows, is also distorted. Nevertheless, the silence is there and is unbearable.

The Hour of the Wolf sketches an artist obsessed by the memory of his first wife who had shared his private world and intuitive visions. Without her, he is lost. His second wife is unable to enter his dark nights of the soul, and he feels utterly alone. Again, there is only silence, his inner world is fractured and he becomes insane. In order to illustrate his thesis, the director employs dreamlike techniques that are sometimes ugly and lacerating but nevertheless keep on touching the real world. The artist obviously does not know who or where he is, and one result of his confusion of reality with illusion is to make the viewer by no means confident of who or where he is.

In my childhood, Bergman says, "I entertained my friends with tremendous stories of my secret exploits. They were embarrassing lies which failed hopelessly when confronted with the level-headed skepticism of the world around me. Finally, I withdrew and kept my dream world to myself. A child looking for human contact, obsessed by his imagination, had been quickly transformed into a hurt, cunning and suspicious day-dreamer." It need not be a far remove from daydream to nightmare nor occasionally from reality to illusion where nothing seems real any more.

It is also in this film that Bergman, fascinated by demons, attempts to actualize them. During the writing of the script, he could not sleep because of the presence of demons in his room. He wrote, "They were there! All of them. And I had difficulty to select them. They would come, all of them, about fifty or sixty of them. . . . I couldn't sleep there because they were there. . . . Yes, they wouldn't get out!" It was Baudelaire who is reputed to have remarked that when devils are called, they come.

A Passion exhibits another artist who perceives himself as a failure and like an anchorite withdraws from further emotional engagements into a cell of physical hard work. His identity is shattered by the shards of despair and confusion, and he concludes that to be both alive and honest is impossible; the only honesty is in silence. The concept of spiritual starvation on account of the death of God and the various ways in which we endeavor to disguise it is again explored. Anna asks, "What is this deadly poison that corrodes the best in us, leaving only the shell?"

The Touch shows yet again Bergman's concern with the question of God's silence. An archaeologist excavating an ancient church discovers a wooden Madonna and Child only to find that, because of its exposure to the light throughout the centuries, wood larvae have eaten away the statue from the inside. Is not Bergman at this place a victim of twentieth-century reductionism, that life is nothing but matter in motion? I think this is borne out by his introduction to *Wild Strawberries:* "Philosophically, there is a book that was a tremendous experience for me: Eiono Kaila's *Psychology of the Personality.* His thesis that man lives strictly according to his needs—negative and positive—was shattering to me but terribly true. And I built on this ground."

Cries and Whispers, also in the vein of a morality play, discloses three sisters and their female servant alone in a house. They are waiting for one of the sisters to die. Perhaps this film is the most exposed and vulnerable statement Bergman has yet made. Man's alienation from God and his fellow man is total. It is a tale of separation, agony and emptiness, of "constant misery and torment." And Karin crescendoes the urgency of the knight's cry in *The Seventh Seal* to the despair and finality of "It's all a tissue of lies," which, repeated several times, becomes almost a refrain. **75**

In one scene the pastor prays over the dead Agnes: "If it is so that you meet God over there in the other land; if it is so that He turns His face toward you; if it is so that you can speak the language that this God understands; if it is so that you can speak to this God, if it is so, pray for us. . . . Ask Him to free us at last from our anxiety, our weariness and our profound doubt. Ask Him for a meaning to our lives. . . ." In his diary, in which I believe he is projecting his own feelings, Bergman has written about a friend: "His glance is forever trying to pierce through the darkness. He is forever trying to catch the sound of a reply to his terrified questions and despairing prayers. But the silence is complete." And Bergman's glance, through the camera, endeavors to pierce the darkness and break the silence. For all such men, there is indeed a tension between what man is told he is and what he knows he is. This brilliant, abrasive film prompts the question: Where can Bergman go from here?

Man, told that he is a puppet, revolts against his puppetdom yet is existentially crushed by his "ironic despair at the Russian roulette of existence." But modern man has an even greater tension: He does not know what to do with what he knows he is; he has no objective framework into which to fit his uniqueness. Bergman sums up his position: "It is my opinion that art lost its basic creative drive the moment it was separated from worship. It severed an umbilical cord and now lives its own sterile life, generating and degenerating itself. In former days the artist remained unknown and his work was to the glory of God. . . . Today the individual has become the highest form and the greatest bane of artistic creation. . . . The individualists stare into each other's eyes and yet deny the existence of each other. . . ." Such people do not know what to do with what they are because they live in a world Bergman portrays, a world of alienation and angst that is noisy with silence, a world where routine is the only sanity. The knight in *The Seventh Seal* speaks for modern man: "Why can't I kill God? . . . Why in spite of everything is He a baffling reality I can't shake off?"

the occult: the religion of the other

Bergman finds God silent, yet in some sense he hears noise from the realm of the demonic. As Chesterton pointed out, when men abandon belief in God they do not believe in nothing but in anything. If God is not real, that does not eliminate His Satanic Majesty.

Nonetheless, so far few directors have ventured into the dangerous and diffused world of the occult. From an earlier epoch, *The Turn of the Screw* perhaps started the trickle, and the significance of *Juliet of the Spirits* should not be overlooked. But it was not until Polanski's *Rosemary's Baby* that the dam burst on the cinema-going public and they were once more made aware of this fact, though few took it seriously. Witchcraft is again to the fore in *The Devil's Own*. Polanski's *Macbeth* makes the most of what Shakespeare gives us in this area, but two recent arrivals, *The Devils* and *The Possession*

The Exorcist (1973), William Friedkin

of Joel Delaney are more refined. Russell's pièce de resistance, *The Devils,* based on historical events in the religious community of Loudun in France in 1634, is a warning "dark as Erebus" of "the palpable obscure." *The Possession of Joel Delaney* is a chilling foray into Satanism, while *The Other* deals with ominous shades from "the other side." *Hair* represents a heyday for horoscopic exploration and superstition. *Don't Look Now,* employing original visual metaphors, partially explores the world of the medium, while *The Devil's Daughter* takes a sensational look at some of the sinister realities to be found in the unseen world.

But it is left to *The Exorcist,* which despite some sensationalism is not a horror film, to grip the reality of the unseen world like a tourniquet, revealing the terror of demon possession. The film has created quite a stir. Perhaps more sense and nonsense have been proclaimed from paper, periodical, pulpit and platform concerning *The Exorcist* than any other film of recent years. One reviewer sees both the book and the film as expressing a "nineteenth-century vision of a world in which modern medicine, psychiatry and criminal science were prophetically unequal to solving life's riddles." Another reviewer says that the film is "hard-core pornography . . . that uses the human fear of evil to create an emotional response and then provides a completely impossible solution." A third calls it a "lurid, sensational horror film that exploits deep-rooted religious sensibilities."

The firm basis in reality that the film possesses is discounted by such criticism, criticism that is committed to a world view that stresses the uniformity of natural causes in a closed system, that allows no room for spiritual reality of any kind, and no room for significant decisions and actions even on man's part. Ultimately such a view is unable to find either a correct explanation for occult activity or a solution to the problem such activity inevitably brings. I would refer such reviewers to the account of a demon-possessed man in the New Testament (Luke 5) and his deliverance.

Likewise, talk of the film as "revealing a widely shared effort to redress psychic imbalance" says nothing and means nothing. It is a classic instance of semantic mysticism, a situation common enough among film reviewers and one which will be taken up in a later chapter.

78

But one question remains: Why is *The Exorcist* so powerful? It is powerful, I believe, precisely because the expectation of the viewers is not satisfied. Most film-goers expect that the film will eventually explain demon possession on naturalistic grounds. But it does not. Rather, the film alerts us to the fact that spiritual evil is a reality within history, that it is a part of the human predicament, not a remote metaphysical speculation. Evil exists as a spiritual reality. Moreover, evil is personal and, when concentrated through occult activity, it may reach a peak of intensity within one or more human beings.

Some people are not ready to accept such a conclusion. The strength of the reality of such evil overcomes them. In fact, the hysterical public reaction to the film is more alarming than the film itself because it tells us something about our own spiritual insight as a society. After *The Exorcist* was released in late 1973, newspapers were filled with accounts of vomiting in cinemas, fainting and psychic shock. One man drove home after the film and then had to return. He had left his wife at the cinema! Psychiatrists reported an influx of calls from people who, after seeing the film, believed they were possessed. Such extreme reactions ought to lead us to the balance suggested by C. S. Lewis: "There are two equal and opposite errors into which our race can fall about the devils. One is to disbelieve in their existence. The other is to believe and then feel an excessive and unhealthy interest in them. They themselves are equally pleased by both errors and hail a materialist or a magician with the same delight."

Possibly, however, the distinction of *The Exorcist* is to placard the fact that, despite psychology and philosophy, modern man does not know how to handle what bubbles up from the subconscious. Denying the existence of true moral guilt and at the same time plagued by guilt feelings, he is unable to deal with either on naturalistic or humanistic grounds.

Yet in films we find traditional Christianity, which is capable of handling both true moral guilt and guilt feelings, spurned and mocked. The weird and sensational, the cultic and demonic, are brought to the fore and taken seriously. One wonders, what next?

Still, it should not be imagined that all contemporary films are **79** deliberate models for or images of man. By no means is this the case. Although it would appear to be a prime concern of today's directors to provide such models, there is a great deal to enjoy, consider and assimilate as well as a number of films that are just plain fun.

Belle de Jour (1968), Louis Bunuel   *Satyricon* (1969), Federico Fellini

cinematic danger points

7

The Exorcist raises a number of questions. How far should a film go in revealing the horror of man at his extremity? When is the audience being merely manipulated, orchestrated like a symphony at the will of a composer and conductor, a script writer and director? When is mind control, that is, the mind control of a director over his audience, a danger? Is it possible so to distort the image of man on film that the film-goer may lose his grasp on his own identity? And why are such trends as these taking place? These are the issues to which we now turn.

mind control: the new propaganda

It is difficult to predict and dangerous to prophesy the future direction of the cinema. Prior to the year 2000, no one can foretell what the accelerative thrust of communications technology will produce. For example, it is possible that stills, speeded up to telescope the life and times of Henry VIII or the assassination of President John F. Kennedy, may develop and have a considerable mesmeric effect on the viewer. It is possible that audio-visual cassettes may be made available for use in the cinema or in one's home. Perhaps televised films will be delivered into the cinema or one's home by cable. It is possible that cinemas may be built containing two, three or even four screens in the same auditorium, all simultaneously projecting different films. In several pavilions at the Montreal World's Fair in 1967, split and multi-screen films were simultaneously projected.

It is also possible that three-dimensional images called holograms may be adapted for use in the cinema in such a way as, on account of audience participation, to create a subliminal, hypnotic effect on the viewer. If this actualizes, mind control will be a reality, and film could become a valuable tool in the hands of manipulators. An elite might regard it as a gift from the gods. In the past, films have been used for propaganda and counter-propaganda, but these were recognizable as such. One thinks of Nazi Germany's two powerful films, *Germany, Awake!* (deliberately designed to send her to sleep) and *Triumph of the Will.* Both were intended to stifle the nation's **82** capacity for independent thought. Future films of the kind described will not be so recognizable.

Another possibility is the use of brain-wiring, which could give each viewer sensations of a transcendental or hallucinatory nature, perhaps confuse fact with fantasy, induce a trance-like effect, break down moral defenses and loosen the viewer's hold on reality. Already one reviewer has pointed out something like this with reference to *A Clockwork Orange:* "I think the film's success in deploying a controlled dream to spirit its own fearful vision past our defenses partly accounts for the extreme reactions to it from some quarters." It is possible that the cinema of the future may reflect a development of the *Happening* or the *Environment* (foreshadowed in the Art Zero, Art Nul exhibition in Amsterdam in 1965). In *Fahrenheit 451,* the acme of affluence is not two or three cars but a three- or four-wall video set that enables a family to become involved in a televised soap opera that might continue for months, a cycle-drama that will simulate the real with the illusory. Communications technology today is such that these could easily become features of cinema. *The Conversation* points toward some of the wonders and dangers in this area.

The dangers are obvious: Unless the viewer's mind is free consciously to be used as a sieve or grid, then there is no way he can understand what is true and what is not. Nor can he know whether the world he is experiencing is real or not. In fact, he cannot even know whether he himself exists or not. If these or similar potential developments come to pass, then not only will there need to be a new definition of what constitutes entertainment in the cinema, but we will have to question whether film is an art form truly defining man in his human condition. Films emphasizing the subliminal and hallucinatory could have serious psychological consequences for the viewer and diminish his critical faculties and moral awareness.

A reviewer of *A Clockwork Orange* seconds this judgment:

But I think [the film] hits its audience at a deeper level of consciousness than mere curiosity.... "With an eloquent command of the medium," wrote one critic, Patrick Snyder-Scumby, "[Kubrick] has created a dream in which he asks us to laugh at his nightmares."... For anyone who views a story as being in the nature of a "controlled dream" is bound to pay regard to the unconscious feelings of a cinema audience, since it is in the unconscious that the dream operates with most potency. *A Clockwork Orange* is nearer this dream state than any film Kubrick has made. Its lighting, editing, photography and especially its music—for sound reaches deeper into the unconscious than even sight—are all combined with events in themselves bizarre and frightening.... We are assailed by a field of forces impossible to repel. *2001: A Space Odyssey,* in a rough sense, was a film whose imagery we were invited to accept, explore and enjoy for the sensuous experiences it conveyed. *A Clockwork Orange,* on the other hand, is one whose images we throw up our hands to ward off.

This reviewer's comments illustrate again the powerful nature of the medium. But, like similar statements, it should not be used as material for prejudgment.

I think that films of the future will certainly develop in these areas but that they will not comprise the totality of films produced. I also think that in the future the film industry may become increasingly aggressive, claiming more and more freedom from censorship and control, both because of its claim to be a superior art form and because of its employment by an elite.

In this overall connection, it is worth noting a straw in the wind. A short time ago it was reported that a Hollywood actress had been offered several million dollars if in one scene in a film she would permit herself to be stabbed. If this kind of thing comes to be accepted, it will be no time before an actor's family is offered millions more for him actually to be killed. As Dostoevsky said, "If there is no God, then everything is permitted." One consequence is that an inordinate thirst for stimulation, sensation and novelty can monopolize man who, having himself become a piece of machinery, treats others as a piece of machinery. Is this not, like a preview to *1984*, one of the truths revealed in *A Clockwork Orange*?

A further disturbing development involves trends in children's films. The Saturday morning children's cinema has largely been replaced by Saturday morning children's TV films. Formerly, such films were fairy or fantasy stories that moved into real life, got the children involved and gave them some sort of an answer to the problems raised. Now the situation is different. The children are just as involved, but they seem to be presented with sophisticated situations and with *adult* problems. Not only are they quite unable to solve these problems, but no answers are given. Children should never be presented with adult problems, nor with exposure to anything that will rob them of the love, security and childlike experiences to which they are entitled.

underground films: surrealism and sanity

In general, we have been considering feature films that at present are shown on the public cinema circuit. But we must not omit the wide variety of "sub-cult" films of today's intellectual, beat and "hip-fringe" society, remarkable films such as Mekas' *Guns of the Trees*, Larcher's *Mare's Tail* and Robert Kramer's *In the Country*. Not only are "mainstream" films supplemented by foreign, documentary, art and sex films, but in addition there are films made to appeal to specialist groups in society. *The Last American Hero* is for stock-car racing enthusiasts and there are films for hot-rodders, surfers and those with a gay problem. These offer little to other than a small coterie.

But there is also an area of film making that is underground. Technology has made hand cameras and video-tape equipment available for general use, and a number of amateurs and students are producing their own films. Some have a certain merit and artistic potential; some are individualized and brash.

One area of avant-garde film making, however, is both underground and experimental. If I may presume to prophesy, these films before long will be part of the standard fare available in the public cinema. They are light years away from that to which we are already accustomed. Indeed, they make one feel like a beleaguered representative of sanity in a dotty world! A basic surrealism with its dreamlike quality exerts a hypnotic effect on the viewer; invariably the camera work is superb and the effects startling.

Pat O'Neill's *Down Wind* is strange and dreamlike. Gunvor Nelson's *My Name Is Oona* has this same quality with the vestiges of a story attached to rather than forming the basis of the film. Her film *Fog Pumas* transfers dreams onto film and as a result transforms the film into dreams. The surrealist characteristic of nothing being real is fundamental to most of these films, which to date are short and designed to affect one in a staccato burst of flashing frames. All is phantasmagoria conveyed in telegrammatic breathlessness; speed is the essence and sound the core. *One and the Same*—the title is significant—is a roller-coasting optical romp. *Schmeerguntz*, a clever piece of Women's Lib apologia, animates, as it were, the paintings of Salvador Dali and de Chirico; its mystical nature is disturbing. There is a subtle amalgam of mysticism and sensuousness in *Moonspool* where the viewers see a naked female body in water, floating, posturing, flowing, weaving, gleaming. Another film of Gunvor Nelson's is *Take Off*; a woman slowly gyrating slowly undresses herself. For this we are prepared. But we are not prepared for what follows: To the accompaniment of fierce sounds and lights incessantly flashing in unison, she disembodies herself. A recent review stated that "what it [the film] says sinks into the watcher's subconscious and stays there." But this is not so because all that drops into the subcon-

85

scious works away there, creating attitudes of mind and determining conduct.

All that has so far been said about the medium and the message is even more applicable to these films. Gunvor Nelson has said, "I try to make my introversions universal," and it would seem that for the woman in *Take Off*, emptiness and absurdity, fear and despair, are the universal realities. It has been said that this type of film is therapeutic. But one must ask what is meant by that. For whom is it therapeutic and for what purpose? The scenes of the woman disembodying herself speak of irrationality and alienation and prompt the question, "What has become of Man?" Surely self-disembodiment is not self-affirmation!

by-passing the will of actor and audience

A third danger point derives from Bresson's observation that "films can be made only by by-passing the will of those who appear in them, using not what they do but what they are." In one sense, this is Symbolism transferred to the screen. As the poet Valéry appeared to regret having to employ language, almost patronizing the verbal medium, so film director Bresson would appear to diminish, if not dispense with, the role of actor *qua* actor. As we have seen, this essentially is because the camera does the acting and the actor submits to its direction. In principle, there is no objection to this. The objection rather is twofold: What may it do to the actor? What may it do to the viewer?

In Losey's *The Go-Between* one wonders what is the effect on the young boy who is involved in the scene of fornication in a hayloft. Or what effect did their involvement in certain scenes have on the adolescent in Mulligan's *Summer of '42*, the boy in *The Heart Murmur*, the boys in *The Cowboys*, the fourteen-year-old girl in *The Exorcist*, the young women in a film depicting a religious community who in one scene were required to masturbate, or those cast for parts in *Pink Flamingoes*? Bertolucci, speaking of *Last Tango in Paris*, said, "Even Marlon Brando was wiped out by the end of the shooting of the film. Without bitterness he told me, 'I was completely and utterly violated by you. I will never make another film like that.'"

Directors cannot be unaware of the psychological effects on those required to perform actions beyond their understanding or experience. This is especially important in the case of children or adolescents whose minds are susceptible to impressions of all kinds.

As far as the effect on the viewer is concerned, two points may be made, and both of these are based on an incontrovertible principle regarding any art form: There is no such thing as a neutral medium. The message, as McLuhan correctly insists, is parallel in importance to the effect of the medium. Because there is no neutral medium or neutral message, there can be no neutral response. A viewer is conditioned subconsciously by both message and medium. Moreover, each viewer is differently affected, privately affected, whether he is aware of it or not. If he is aware of the effect of what he has seen, then at some time he will respond with an attitude of mind that will result in certain conduct. And that conduct, in line with his inclinations, will be entirely a free choice. If he is not aware of the effect of what he has seen, his subsequent actions may be to some extent manipulated, that is, not a result of free and conscious choice.   **87**

Second, many contemporary films have the effect of turning the viewer into a voyeur. When the actor, responding to the camera, becomes an exhibitionist, the viewer has little alternative to becoming a voyeur. In effect, this is the case with films like *Trash* and *Last Tango in Paris*. In films of this kind the blue-movie club has taken over the public cinema. Perhaps Marcel Duchamp pointed the way with his picture in a room behind the gallery that has to be observed through a peephole.[1]

why films are produced

Why are so many directors making the types of film we have been discussing? There are a number of reasons, I think. The first is that, regarding cinema as an art form, directors correctly believe it is both necessary and legitimate to feel their way toward new philosophic and technical expressions; furthermore, they want to reflect and promote interest in current issues. This involves probing for audience reaction and response. To some extent, the audience on occasion may be regarded as an object under a microscope. Honest directors are exploring modern man's dilemma in order to discover whether there is a valid solution and, if so, where it lies. It is often falsely assumed that because directors have their own axes to grind —and one does not necessarily have to be dishonest or negative to grind an axe—their integrity is suspect. I would strongly deplore any suggestions of this kind. Such men, in common with many, have lost their way in the world, but that ought not to expose them to condemnation but to compassion. Only their work is to be criticized.

A second reason is that some directors faithfully live in the light of their left-wing, or at least non-traditional or anti-Establishment, beliefs. I think it is true to say that some have a definite policy of mocking the best in current culture, softening it up, maybe hoping to take over the reins and establish a new way of life. Far be it from me to imagine a communist skeleton in every cupboard, but neither am I naive enough to believe that left-wing tactics are confined to the open and legitimate and not to fifth-column activity.

Associated with this is a third reason; some directors for sociological rather than political reasons wish to "liberate" society from its allegedly vestigial, outmoded Puritan and outworn Victorian mores. Fellini commented on *Satyricon*: "Rome in its decline was quite similar to our world today. There was the same fury of enjoying life, the same lack of moral principles and ideologies and the same complacency. Today we are finished with the Christian myth and aware of a new one. There is an analogy in *Satyricon*." This view would seem to extend into more and more areas of the entertainment world and cultural activities.

A fourth reason is the profit motive. Films have to sell internationally, and financiers expect a consistent return on their investment. Once this is assured, with the near certainty of a wide and lengthy market, there is plenty of money to be made by numbers of people when a film under distinguished direction is produced. One aspect of this is the "consumer-market" approach. *Love Story, Last Tango in Paris, The Exorcist, The Great Gatsby,* among others, considerably increased their "sales" because they aroused great anticipation. The premiere of each was announced weeks beforehand through lavish advertising. When the actual event took place, seats had to be booked. Queues formed and interest soared.

We should realize in this connection that communications technology is still in its infancy, and film is going to become a paramount part of the octopus-like communications development within society that is already past the experimental stage. All areas of living, it is projected, will be linked together through a kind of "total communication." Surely, today's directors cannot be unaware of tomorrow's consumer market.

There is a fifth reason which might seem to be in the realm of fantasy, but I do not think it is. As I mentioned before, when the concept of *absolute truth* is abandoned, men and women do not then believe in nothing (though philosophically nihilism does result), they believe in anything. "Anything goes" is a tenet of anarchism. Thousands of today's generation are involved in an international, idealized revolt against injustice and affluence in its various forms, and many of them are prepared to fight for anarchy. They rub the Aladdin's lamp of revolt and hope that the genie of Che Guevara, Fanon and Marcuse will appear. Such natural idealism may be **89** channeled into anger and destruction and finally into destruction for its own sake, thus involving pleasure in violence and in the infliction of pain. If the occasional expression of this in some films is not intentional, then it is there by default. In any event, the content of a film may sometimes become material for promoting anarchy.

For whatever reason, film makers are toying with techniques that open the way for mind control, they are redefining man so that his insanity becomes sanity, and they are frequently by-passing the wills of both actor and audience. Therefore, it becomes increasingly important that thinking men and women sound more than occasional alarm when danger points are reached and provide for the larger society guidelines and safeguards. In other words, as viewers we should rapidly develop and use our critical faculties.

Bob and Carol and Ted and Alice (1969), Mazursky   *American Graffiti* (1973), Lucas

censorship or criticism?

It is obvious that sensitive people should develop a critical perspective from which to view developments in film. Too much is at stake to adopt a wait-and-see attitude. Yet we must be careful not to look superficially at a few current films and then launch out in an attitude of censorship.

censorship: marking time with society's norms

Censorship in Great Britain is, by and large, no longer a problem nor even a joke because it is virtually nonexistent. A similar situation appears to obtain in the United States. Don Siegel said recently, "When I was talking to the censors in America about getting a PG (Parental Guidance) rather than an R (Restricted) certificate for *Charley Varrick,* all they were concerned about was blood and sex and violence. Yet I knew that if they just once said, 'Listen, you can't have a PG rating because this film is about people murdering and stealing and getting away with it and is therefore immoral,' I'd have been dead. I couldn't have argued against that. But the subject never came up. That shows how sick the whole idea of censorship is." As long ago as 1963, French film director Roger Vadim remarked, "I make sexy pictures only because they are easier to get past the French censorship than pictures about almost any other subject."

Originally, censorship was confined to blasphemy and was later extended to cover obscenity, but all the films mentioned hitherto have been passed by the British Board of Film Censors and received graded certificates. But the British genius for compromise and ambiguity has provided a complicating factor in that occasionally the British Board of Film Censors does not have the last word. A body such as, for example, the Greater London Council or any local town council may reject a film the British Board has passed and pass a film the British Board has rejected. Recently, the British Board rejected *Manson* but the Greater London Council, whose writ runs throughout the City of London and into bordering parts of the Home Counties, passed it.

There was a time when society had its taboos and viewers their prejudices, and the censors marched in time with both, but today censorship is only approximate and usually ineffective. It is vigorously opposed on three grounds. First, it smacks of Establishment authority; second, it curbs freedom of expression in seeking to reflect and promote thought-forms and lifestyles; and third, it limits films in a way theaters are not limited because there is no longer any viable theater censorship. *Oh! Calcutta!* for several years has been allowed to deprave theater audiences, but it is only a matter of months since it was permitted to corrupt cinema viewers.

As far as the plea for freedom of expression is concerned, this is a return to Art for Art's sake; however it is disguised, the ultimate humanist appeal is always to this. Northrop Frye has written that "Art for Art's sake is a retreat from criticism which ends in an impoverishment of civilized life itself. The only way to forestall the work of criticism is through censorship which has the same relation to criticism that lynching has to justice." In other words, there is a free association of ideas in criticism and justice, just as there is an association between censorship and lynching. Frye seems to be saying that for criticism to guide is fair, but for criticism to guard is not so fair. This attitude is exemplified in a review of *The Devil in Miss*

Jones: "Never has such an imbecilic bit of trash inspired so much thoughtful criticism. . . . This film, like all junk films, should be protected for the consenting adult, but the critic who protects it by talking about the quality of the photography or by saying how unerotic it is, is missing the point. A dirty movie *should* be erotic."

By no means should any portrait be false, but neither does each character need to spill all his thoughts, words and actions over the viewer before he arrives at an understanding of himself or of society. This is especially important in the case of those who are unable to protect themselves from exploitation. At this place, an external control of some kind is required. The law should be more explicit without detailing minutiae, thus possibly providing a director with a little more form within which to exercise his freedom. Another help to discriminating viewers would be a clear, unsensational synopsis of the film story displayed in the foyer of each cinema.

In the last analysis, the most effective form of censorship is to keep your money in your pocket. No one is compelled to go to a film, and a refusal on the part of a community to attend a certain film— **93** provided first the film is really known and understood and the boycott therefore is on principle and not on prejudice—is one of the best forms of censorship.

criticism: semantic dishonesty

In general terms, it has been argued that the best censorship is film criticism itself, for it can provide both encouragement and deterrence. On the face of it, this seems reasonable, but it tends to break down in practice. A film review of part of *The Heart Murmur,* in which a fifteen-year-old boy commits incest with his mother, reads as follows: "The moment takes its truth from the reciprocal sympathy between the young Italian matron and the youngest and most sensitive of her sons." Is this fair criticism? The reviewer has used soft connotation words, without reference to their semantic meaning, in order to squeeze out moral judgment. This is both dishonest and pernicious.[1] It is not unusual to find words such as *honest, controversial, beautiful, truthful, commitment, sincere, realistic* employed sometimes without any reference to their original and still understood semantic meaning. *Cactus Flower,* although endorsing a relativistic view of marriage, ironically points up the dangers when words are used so as to lose their semantic meaning.

In all areas we are experiencing a "retreat from the word" as that which brings the mind into accord with reality. Sterne in his novel *Tristram Shandy* maintained that words "express the person who gives them utterance but no other thing," and this idea obviously holds much attraction for man living in an apparently meaningless world. If the world is meaningless, why should words mean anything? So comes today's semantic mysticism where it is maintained that words, as we see, are not important but are symbols only for subjective states.

A critique of the writer William Burroughs illustrates this. When this critique was written, Burroughs was a self-confessed drug addict, alcoholic and a man with a gay problem. Paul Bowles wrote of him as follows: "His life had no visible organization in it but knowing he was an addictive type he had chosen that way of giving himself an automatic interior discipline which was far more rigorous than any he could have imposed on himself objectively." Another writer, Alan Ansen, spoke of Burroughs' position regarding "the need for commitment": "This commitment he finds in addiction to narcotics. . . . A deeply committed personality. . . . He is an indispensable indication that it is possible to be vicious without being slack. . . . To use drugs without losing consciousness or inarticulateness, to love boys without turning into a mindless drab is a form of heroism. . . . Burroughs' attitude towards property is most austere."[2] This type of urbane, amoral criticism is frequently to be found among reviewers. Beyond doubt, if words mean anything at all, there is here a perversion of language because debauchery not only is glamorized but made to appear positive and virtuous. "The shallow conception of mysterious eroticism triumphant over morality and restraint is glamorized by the bogus sacredness of perverted religiosity, which does not hesitate to abuse the traditional vocabulary of chivalrous romanticism and even of Christian morality."[3] Bowles' and Ansen's critiques are prime illustrations of linguistic legerdemain.

One who did not write in this vein, however, is Anthony Lejeune who, in part of a review of *Last Tango in Paris,* wrote, "The constant obscenities and the perversions are the whole point of the film. . . . It corrupts and wastes the talents of the undoubtedly gifted people who produced it. It corrupts the film industry which puts it out as entertainment. . . . *Last Tango in Paris* would sure be a good place to call a halt."

Honest criticism of this kind is to be welcomed. And in itself it is a form of censorship. But it lacks a moral imperative, and the onus on such courageous writers is to provide a basis for their criticism. On what basis and for what reason should a halt be called?[4] Ethical imperatives have capitulated to the captains of industry, but that does not mean that a citizen passively accepts the status quo. One reason is enough: "When bad men combine," wrote Burke, "the good must associate else they will fall one by one, an unpitied sacrifice in a contemptible struggle." In other words, the quickest way to insure the control of total relativism and permissiveness is for the silent majority to do nothing.[5]

There is, thus, another form of censorship—that of lawful protest, protest that is informed, positive, fair and continual. Such censorship is not only a Christian duty but a civic responsibility. Picketing the cinema, writing to the press, holding a seminar, writing to one's Congressman or Member of Parliament—these are some specific things that may be done.

the criteria of excellence

Prior to censorship or criticism, however, is the question of criteria for assessing the merits of a film. Basically there are three: form, validity and content. All three are criteria for each art form. A painter as well as a film director may be judged on these criteria. From time to time one or the other of them may vary, but that does not necessarily invalidate the whole achievement. Taking the whole of a director's work into account, one is able to say that such and such a director is a fine or a great artist.

By *form* is meant that a film is to be assessed on the quality of its script, casting, acting, location, camera work, lighting, color, sound, mixing, dubbing and editing.

By *validity* is meant that a film is to be assessed on whether the director is true to his world view and whether this world view is consistent with his other portrayals. One has to ask if the director is making his film for the benefit of the critics or for a group in or a section of society or solely for money. If the film is for any sectional or personal interest, then one may doubt its validity.

By *content* is meant that a film is to be assessed on the relative truth or falsity of the overall philosophical statements it makes. This is a particularly important criterion on account of the advances made and being made in cinematographic and communications technology. Achieving first-class criteria of form and validity, so powerful a medium may be enabled to get away with murder in content. The richness of the frame and the high quality of the canvas often blind the viewer to the tormented nature of the painting.

Certainly, a film is not to be assessed on the basis of Art for Art's sake: "Look at this, listen to that, simply for the experience." This is still an underlying concept in cultural and aesthetic areas for several reasons, not least because such a view frees a director or writer from any consideration of moral values. To adapt Oscar Wilde's famous aphorism, "There is no such thing as a moral or an immoral film; films are either well directed or badly directed." This issues in the absolute independence of art from content and morality, and it emphasizes perfection of form independent of validity and content. To evaluate art on this basis not only tends to exclude the three objective criteria that serve as reasonable yardsticks, but also invites a subjective viewpoint on all other matters, and that leaves one without any yardstick at all. It means that Art becomes self-affirming, autonomous, an end in itself.

When art becomes the self-affirmation of the artist and is declared to be a means of inner transformation, then what began as Art for Art's sake further deteriorates into Art to transform man. This is illustrated by Henry Miller who insists in religious terminology and with religious fervor that the artist is the one from whom all life flows. Leonard Bernstein speaks for the musician when he says, "The concert hall is a sacred house and in it the artist will continue to create you, Father and you, me." The composer Stockhausen in a recent interview said, "Music is a means to a new aware-ness; music will transform people." Even Herbert Marcuse espouses this philosophy when he asserts that "art will be an integral factor in shaping the quality and appearance of things, in shaping the reality, the way of life."[6] These statements are a natural extension of the observation of an earlier romantic, Shelley, when he said that "poets are the unacknowledged legislators of the world."

This philosophy is a cul-de-sac, not a main road, and leads from the moral twilight of do-your-own-thing on into a spiritual wilder-ness. "Art for Art's sake" should be inscribed over what Coleridge called "The dread watch-tower of man's absolute self."

It is beyond the purposes of the present discussion to develop these criteria. I would recommend that the reader consult other more technical treatises on film in regard to the first criterion, *form*. Concerning *validity*, general works on aesthetics may provide a guide. I do wish, however, to consider the third criterion and will do so in the following chapter. At this point I wish to insist on one thing: What has been said so far should be something on which both Chris- **97** tians and many non-Christians can agree. Regardless of the content of one's moral convictions, films will challenge and threaten them. To be aware of this is simply to be more fully human and conscious of one's dignity as a man or woman. Still, I wish to go further and suggest ways Christians can develop a specifically Christian attitude to the cinema.

Last Year at Marienbad (1962), Alain Resnais   *The Virgin Spring* (1960), Ingmar Bergman

developing a
christian perspective

In film, one is confronted with an expression of God's creativity in and through man, whether those involved are aware of it or not. The basis for a Christian assessment of any art form is that the God of the Bible has put creativity akin to his own into his creation. This gift in others is thankfully to be received and then responsibly evaluated by the criteria suggested.

There should, moreover, be no surprise if one's own philosophy of life is not reflected in any given film, because it is film's business, as it is that of literature, to influence the viewpoint, if not modify the vision, of the viewer through recording the experiences of others. At the same time, questions must be asked: What are the postulates behind the film? On what view of man is it based? What is its criterion of humanness? What understandings of truth emerge? What moral or intellectual somersaults has the director made? These questions may be asked of any of the visual or verbal arts.

two basic ground rules

Each viewer, whether he is a Christian or not, must form his own personal, thought-out convictions concerning any film he sees. Because there is no such thing as a neutral medium or a neutral response, anything less than this may temporarily "wipe him out" and ultimately throw him into confusion. No film should be viewed simply for viewing's sake or because there is nothing better to do. This results in uncritical and passive viewing and exposes the viewer to certain dangers. As I have said, one's critical faculties should never be left at the box office.

First, a film-goer should not let himself be bombarded by suave criticism. He must not let himself be bulldozed into regarding cinema or any other art form as beyond technical, aesthetic and moral judgment. Man lives in a moral universe created by a moral God and to say so is to swim against the cultural stream. Yet the Christian should not only see films but assess them according to the criteria suggested and according to a biblical mentality and not, in the main, according to the criteria admitted by existential directors and critics. Unless the mind is free consciously to be used as a sieve or a grid, there is no way one can understand what is true or know whether the world one is experiencing is real or not.

Second, in view of the continued blurring of the distinction between illusion and reality in a number of contemporary films, it will become increasingly crucial to keep the mind fully engaged. It is no accident that many people refer to the world as a "madhouse" or that films like *Stop the World, I Want to Get Off* and *It's a Mad, Mad, Mad World* are made. Nor is it surprising to find *Morgan* depicting life inside a mental hospital as superior to life outside it. In the final scene of *Blow-Up*, the tennis players hit a non-existent ball to and fro over the net, thus symbolizing the hero's acceptance of either the unreal (and irrational) or the real (and rational) and his inability to distinguish between them. Who knows how many viewers identify with the hero in that scene! Other films already mentioned break down this distinction between illusion and reality and the cause-and-effect relationships between these two realms, thus tending to cause confusion in the viewer's mind as to what constitutes reality and identity, not only in terms of the film but in terms of the viewer's own life.

Films are made not only to affect the senses but to grip the imagination, which then sets up an attitude of mind and in turn produces certain emotions leading to certain conduct. As we have seen, film forces its way into the citadel of beliefs and feelings. Moreover, as in advertising, each image tends to ignite the physical conditions and conduct corresponding to it. At drive-ins, for example, what is acted out on the screen is sometimes lived out in the car.

In watching a succession of flashing frames, the viewer is seeing, as it were, a series of flowing X-rays, and the effect of this on him may be devastating insofar as he becomes unable at any moment during the performance to gather his wits in order to appraise what is happening, not so much on the screen as to himself. And with the possibility in the cinema of the future of altering one's mental state, this danger is not to be minimized.[1] The creation and staging of specialized psychological experiences in super-Disneylands in which the cinema will play its full role may be expected. This will be poles apart from that with which we are already familiar.

It might be inferred from what I have just said that a Christian does not go to a cinema to enjoy himself but solely in a critical frame of mind and on the defensive. If this were so, I for one would be sad and disappointed. I hold that one still goes to the cinema to enjoy oneself, to be entertained, that is, to hold apart the routine world in order to engage in something different. There is so much to be uncovered and learned about the human dilemma from the human experience in films. The slapstick, the sentimental, the satirical, the serious—each, like its counterpart on the stage or on a canvas or in a novel, should be accepted openly and fairly and criticized honestly and objectively. Of course, contemporary films both reflect and promote thought-forms and lifestyles, and most films operate on non-theistic, existential postulates. Yet each one is different and has to be accorded its own contribution and distinctiveness. Moreover, directors, in analyzing the nature of man and the human dilemma, almost inevitably give some insights which are true even from a Christian standpoint. Even when a Christian finds a film's content to be false or misleading, he may praise the director and actors for their creativity and artistry.

the nature of man and the concept of truth

This having been said, however, a Christian should enter the cinema with a solid grasp of who man is and what truth is. By and large today's directors are concerned with man's dilemma and are seeking to give positive insights, even though they invariably view man's problem as metaphysical and not moral.[2] And, as we have observed, experimental underground cinema compels us to see that even this approach is being eroded and man is to be viewed simply as a piece of machinery, functioning in a random universe made by two blind infants, Matter and Chance. The cinema of the future, however, may well see him as this but also manipulate him.

What is the distinctiveness of man? It is this: to be created not in the reflection but in the image of God. This has overwhelming implications. In the first place, man is seen to have God's *rational* image; he is able to consider and then comprehend God's world. Second, man is seen to have God's *moral* image; he is able to apprehend the idea of goodness and morality and to feel a sense of guilt when his

life does not measure up to this idea of goodness. Third, man is seen to have God's image in that he is able to address God through language in meaningful I-You *communication;* he similarly may address himself and his fellowmen. Fourth, man is seen to have God's image in that he is *self-aware;* he is able to explore himself and develop relationships. Fifth, man is seen to have God's image in that he has the capacity to choose to *love* and in turn be loved; he can give himself emotionally and respond to emotion. Sixth, man is seen to have God's image in that he has not only a mind within a body; he is linked with God through his *spirit.* Finally, man is seen to have God's image in that he has *deputed, responsible sovereignty* over God's world; he is able to be a prince-regent. This view of man is vastly different from current theories presented through the contemporary arts, theories based on existentialism with man as a piece of machinery or theories presenting the essence of Eastern thought, that "when man enters the water, he makes no ripple."

The distinctiveness of man is that he alone can say, "Because God is, therefore I am." And not only is man created in God's image but, when he becomes a Christian, he is re-created by God's Holy Spirit.

When a man or a woman really sees himself as lost and as having revolted against God, when he realizes that he is a sinner and then comes to God in repentance (changing his mind about God and himself), seeking and receiving forgiveness through the death of Christ and subsequent new life through the promises of God, then he experiences the re-creation by God's Holy Spirit and comes into a true, beautiful and fulfilling relationship with God through Christ.

In the face of contemporary views of man, it is vital to know, understand and realize the difference of man and the difference it makes. This is not the place to enter into a full-scale discussion about the nature of man. Suffice it to say that it has brilliantly and convincingly been demonstrated, apart from biblical revelation, that man differs radically in kind from the rest of creation, that he performs certain kinds of activities not found at all in other living things or in machines, and that there is some factor in man's make-up that is absent in all other animate and inanimate things.[3]

The cultural consensus of our day, however, stresses not man's uniqueness but the uniformity of man with his environment. In the face of this, we must deny the view of man presented in many contemporary films. We must clearly state the biblical view of man: Because man is created in God's image, he is not a piece of machinery or a no-thing; he is not a complex rat but a significant creature with meaning, identity and purpose. Moreover, the world in which man lives is open to God's entering it at any time and also to man's re-ordering of it. Knowledge is available outside man for it has been provided by God, and man with his God-given intellect can grasp the meaning that God has placed in all created reality around him. Prepared through *general revelation* (the meaning of reality perceivable in the external world), man is also able to receive *special revelation* (the propositional, verbal revelation in the Bible). Because God has made him in his image, man can identify the source of this special revelation as the God of general revelation, the God in whom he lives and moves and has his being. Thus man is by no means self-sufficient, for he is dependent on God who created him. And God has made man to live in an ordered world where everything holds together.[4] Thus the Christian view of man is that God, the infinite-personal God, made the world, made man to live in that world, gave man through revelation true and sufficient knowledge of himself, knowledge of the world and knowledge of man.

The contemporary view of truth is similar to the contemporary view of man. In today's thought-forms, truth is seen as a subjective, relative matter in which, as a recent writer put it, "Thinking makes it so." Truth is a synthesis and encompasses everything, including falsehood, and consequently there is no such thing as non-truth. In addition, Eastern thinking has penetrated Western thought-forms with the Hindu assertion that an awareness of self equals truth. That is, truth is conceived as contentless meditation or pure experience. Imagination, a tenet of the Romantic Movement, is the gateway to truth; ultimate reality is to be found only in experience or via the imagination. One extension of this is that an irrationalism or an anti-rationalism develops and the mind is put into cold storage. Philosophical, religious and cultural emphases today are being stated in terms of the subjective, the irrational, the mystical, the experiential, and their inevitable by-products are the counterfeit, the confused and the contentless.

The biblical view is poles apart. It asserts that truth is conformity to reality, to the reality of that which is; it states what intrinsically *is* in the external world and in man. The Christian has every reason for taking "that which is" to be derived from, created by, "He Who is." And He Who is, the God of the Bible, is an objective reality rooted in the revelation of himself in history.

In the Bible, truth is never seen as something abstract or scholastic. It is impossible to see it as being "confused with a Greek Orthodox ikon, a Salvador Dali painting, psychological truth or the counterfeit infinity produced by hard drugs." Truth, as the Bible proclaims it, is objective and absolute; it has content and can be imparted to man.

Thus, because the God of the Bible is *absolute truth,* the Christian gives no place to subjective or relative views of truth. He recognizes that if the objective basis for reality is removed, a man quickly finds himself unable to distinguish between illusion and reality.[5] Indeed unless there are certain things that are objectively true and not just

Blow-Up (1967), Michelangelo Antonioni

there in my mind, then life has little meaning and intellectual reasoning has less purpose. And if there is no truth, then there is no hope.

The twin glories of the biblical system are, first, that *absolute truth* is rooted in the revelation of God in history and therefore is able to be seen as objectively true, and, second, that through the operation of the Holy Spirit this truth becomes a personal, subjective, moment-by-moment experience. The Bible speaks constantly of the fact of truth and that it can be known by man. Moreover, it claims to reveal the true nature of man. This is in sharp contrast to the agony of silence or the despair of alienation which modern man is constantly expressing, which Jean-Paul Sartre has expressed as "total responsibility in total solitude."

In the last analysis a Christian should be able to evaluate a film on the basis of *absolute truth* in the person of the God of the Bible. Subjectivism is valueless as a basis for assessment. So is collectivism, a majority opinion based on convenience or necessity; this is only subjectivism to the nth degree and then extended. Nor is there any basis in the building of a stockade of negative biblical texts behind which a Christian may be tempted self-righteously to take his ease. Neither is negative prooftexting of any value. The Bible is not a quarry from which a Christian can dig what he, subjectively, values and then leave the rest as rubble. God has given the Christian no liberty in this matter. Too many Christians are acquainted with what the Bible says, and too few with what it is saying; too many can give chapter and verse for nearly everything and fail to understand the overall purpose and sweep of Scripture. The sole basis for criticism is "the *whole* purpose and plan and counsel of God."

One salient point that emerges when we begin to understand what the whole Bible is saying is this idea of balance. There is a balance in all parts and in all aspects of Scripture. This same balance should be evident in the life of a Christian, and it can be as he lives out the Reformers' cry, "The Word and the Spirit!" The fullness of the Holy Spirit grounded in the balanced truth of Scripture can keep the Christian balanced as he moves along, enjoying and always assessing the thought-forms, lifestyles and arts of the day, and then goes on asking God to make him both light and salt to his generation.

106   A Christian's vocation is first to love God, for only then is a person able to show love for and understanding of those who have lost their way in the world. But, in order to do so, he must know what the Bible is saying, he should have a real understanding of contemporary culture, he needs an apologetic that meets man's postulates and he requires power from the Holy Spirit as he moves among men and women with concern, courage and compassion.[6]

to go or not to go

It is my conviction that a Christian, providing that his foundations are firm, should see films and become involved in the arts and other forms of knowledge. The Lordship of God in Christ must be seen to extend into all areas of life. But there is little point in talking about the gospel being *to* the whole man (body, mind, emotions, spirit, will) *for* the whole man (his daily relationship to God in Christ, his exercising creativity, being fulfilled and becoming a blessing to others) unless the legitimate extensions are understood and accepted. At the same time, whether any given Christian is to go to an art exhibit or to a film is always to be a matter that he decides before God, not one that is laid down for him by anyone else. Moreover, should he become involved beyond the point of being able to keep his priorities right and his intimate, personal relationship with God through Christ open and real, then he had far better retrench and reconsider. It is both wrong and foolish for a Christian thoughtlessly to expose himself and go out on an artistic limb without a full awareness of the issues involved. For some to do so might prove disastrous. For others, it may be safe. But even then only up to a certain point. Each has to find his own level. What a Christian does or sees and when he does or sees it is his responsibility under the leadership of the Holy Spirit, and he should be both sensitive and honest to that leading. There are, as we have seen, dangers; there are also, as we shall see, safeguards.

If we understand the postulates behind modern man's thinking, the dangers are far less. True, the visual is considerably more powerful than the verbal, and it is again necessary to say that there is no neutrality in this particular art form nor indeed in the media generally. But God wants me as light and salt, and he stands by his promises as I choose for him. Yet I should see not only that which reassures or soothes me into feeling that after all the world is more or less in line with my own likes or dislikes. It is not, and to do this is dishonest and stupid. The Christian should watch and think in such a way as lovingly to meet the non-Christian on his own ground. As I have tried to indicate, we should certainly be mistaken if we thought that we had nothing to learn from non-Christian art forms. Most of us at some time watch TV, and so to reject film-going *in toto* is as blinkered as to refuse novel-reading!

At the same time, it is not part of the Christian's business to see and absorb films indiscriminately, to suck up like a vacuum cleaner any philosophic dust or pornographic dirt under the erroneous impression that Truth—undefined—will somehow or other crystallize. Neither is it any part of a Christian's business to be myopic or turn a blind eye to evil. The Christian unequivocally turns his back on evil, but he does not close his eyes to it. Rather, he faces it steadily in his Savior's strength as his Savior did.

Milton, a writer not usually associated with this point of view, spoke strongly in favor of keeping one's eyes open to reality:

"To the pure all things are pure"; not only meats and drinks, but all kinds of knowledge whether good or evil; the knowledge cannot defile, nor consequently the books, if the will and conscience be not defiled.... As therefore the state of man now is, what wisdom can there be to choose, what continence to forbear, without the knowledge of evil? He that can apprehend and consider vice with all her baits and seeming pleasures, and yet abstain, and yet distinguish, and yet prefer that which is truly better, he is the true warfaring Christian.

He then presses the argument home: "I cannot praise a fugitive and cloistered virtue, unexercised and unbreathed, that never sallies out and sees her adversary, but slinks out of the race where that immortal garland is to be run for, not without dust and heat."[7]

The implication of these noble words should be grasped not only for our sake but for our children's. At the end of the century as now, the balance and peace are to be found in the things that cannot be shaken, and the supremacy of that balance is to be found in the uncompromising worldliness of Christ who constantly came into direct contact with sinners and sin, with unbelievers and unbelief, eventually himself becoming sin and remaining untainted. He came into the world which, in Gerard Manley Hopkins' phrase, "wears man's smudge and shares man's smell," and, with concern, courage and compassion, Christ faced, undeflected, the thought-forms and life-styles of his day.

For each of us, part of growing into maturity is acquiring some awareness or knowledge of the sinfulness of man. Some of that knowledge must be acquired vicariously rather than experientially. The cinema doors are open. But we have to choose. The brothel doors are not open, for God has laid an embargo on them as he has in certain other particulars. Still, the Christian has to choose. The will, although fallen, is free. And it appears that a wise awareness of the content of human nature is part of growing into maturity; this is so for all men. From time to time, then, it is possible for God's Holy Spirit to use therapeutically for the Christian a film directed by a non-Christian.

film-going in the light of eternity

As has been said, all truth belongs to God, and fine minds created by
him can discover significant portions of that truth, even though they
may not know its ultimate source. A Christian has to bring all his
film-going to the touchstone of Scripture. As with all knowledge, he
should see it as *sub speciae aeternitatis,* that is, in the light of eternity.
But unless he consciously and tirelessly employs this touchstone, he
may quickly become spiritually anesthetized and intellectually paralyzed. A Christian must never forget one crucial thing: He alone
has true and sufficient knowledge of God and the power for min-
istry through the Holy Spirit in a fallen and abnormal world. He has
to use the knowledge he has, whether that knowledge is of the film
or literature or science, and he has to see it in the light of eternity.
Otherwise his thinking gets out of perspective and his living out of
proportion.

When the true and sufficient knowledge of God that he has been
given is tested at this point, that is, when God's revelation of himself,
man and the external world is perceived to be rational and true **109**
knowledge, then the Christian is able to give to his contemporaries
true knowledge concerning God and film, or whatever it may be.
He can tell them the truth of what they are viewing. Often he may
observe that some of a director's insights are valuable, that he is asking the right questions concerning the reality that is there, but that
he gives an inadequate solution because his philosophy is derelict.
God requires us to use the rational, true knowledge we have been
given, and he requires that we act upon it day by day. If we do not,
the spirit may become a vacuum and the mind an air pocket.

By and large, the Bible alone shows *why* man goes wrong. But the
arts can show *how* man goes wrong. So if a film has something valuable to say concerning the human in the context of the divine, then a
Christian's greatest problem is overcome. The question no longer is,
Should I go to the cinema? but What are my intentions and what
are the safeguards in the cinema-going that I may and ought to un-
dertake? If all film-going is undertaken in an honest, earnest desire
to learn more about the power of God and the plight of man, then
serious film-going has something of value to give.

At the same time, the Christian has to establish a specifically Christian critique over and above that admitted by the non-Christian world. The gulf between a biblical mentality and humanistic thought must be bridged. What is needed is not the "Oh, I don't see that kind of film" attitude but the "Yes, I have seen it and found much of enjoyment and interest there, but its conclusions were bankrupt." Through the Word and the Spirit and with real compassion first for man and then for his plight, a Christian may get alongside his contemporaries in the knowledge that the weapons of our warfare are not physical. Still, these weapons are mighty before God for the overthrow and destruction of strongholds, inasmuch as we refute arguments and theories and reasonings and every proud and lofty thing that sets itself up against the true knowledge of God (2 Cor. 10:4-5).

This line of approach to modern man and to contemporary culture is endorsed by the great biblical scholar J. Gresham Machen who, as long ago as 1912, wrote,

> The Christian cannot be satisfied as long as any human activity is either opposed to Christianity or out of all connection with Christianity. Christianity must pervade not merely all nations but all of human thought. The Christian, therefore, cannot be indifferent to any branch of earnest human endeavor. It must all be brought into *some* relation to the gospel. It must be studied either to be demonstrated as false or in order to be made useful in advancing the Kingdom of God. The Kingdom must be advanced not merely extensively but also intensively. The church must seek to conquer not merely every man for Christ but also the whole of man.[8]

Such has ever been part of the Christian's responsibility, and any retreat into asceticism or monasticism or a false antithesis between mind and spirit is unbiblical.

some final safeguards

The Christian should be in no doubt concerning the dangerous, decadent and destructive forces that are to be found in the arts as elsewhere. He should not be surprised at anything he sees on today's screen. But sometimes he should be shocked if not outraged, and if he is not then it may be because sin has become commonplace and he has lost his sense of the extreme malignity and immeasurable sinfulness of sin (Rom. 7:13). He has to realize that he is as much a deviant in today's society as any political or social extremist or so-called misfit, and his first priority and safeguard is to have a continuously honest and loving, intimate and personal relationship with God through Christ, honoring his Word and being filled with his Spirit. The conjunction of all these will effect a maturing, biblical mentality, a seeing of things from God's point of view.

A Christian's film-going should be balanced by biblical study, contemporary cultural understanding and devotional reading. Before going to the cinema, he ought to read several film reviews, reading between the lines as well. He should be critical in his thinking; one of his chief safeguards is that he develops a mind of his own on these matters. He has to realize also that before long, on account of advances in communications technology, an elite may well capture the total media. And then what is going to be his position? A **111** Christian might well pray before he enters the cinema, and he always should discuss the film with his friends immediately afterwards in order to assess and do justice to the visual images by placing them on the verbal level.

His motives have to remain single-minded. If at times he is watching the erotic or dishonest for its own sake, he should have the moral courage to walk out of the cinema. He should walk out of the cinema in any event if for one reason or another he cannot take any more of the film, especially if he feels something vital is being sucked out of him. Each person's diet is slightly different and he must find what suits him. Each person's level of prurience is likewise different, and there is no sense whatsoever in debilitating one's self. The degree of exposure to overt pornography, whether of sexuality or violence, should be tailored to one's own responses. If a person is overstimulated, his viewing should be carefully observed and assuredly reduced. If he is able to enjoy and critically evaluate a film free from any inner disturbance and, above all, with his personal relationship with God through Christ unimpaired, then he can set his own limits.

During the performance, it is wise and helpful to make notes of passages of dialogue and the significance of images and symbols, and then work through them afterwards, bearing in mind that dialogue, images and symbols have to be seen in the context of the whole film. But this I would repeat: It is essential for Christians to see most contemporary films together and discuss them immediately afterwards, not the following day but before that day is over. Let one's prayers include directors and actors and actresses. Consider making a direct personal approach to a director or actor, either for private conversation or for interview. Or try writing a film review and submitting it to a magazine or local newspaper.

the christian as film maker

Perhaps one of the most urgent matters confronting Christians is to consider what gifts and abilities they may have in this area of the arts and how those gifts may be individually and especially collectively employed. When may we expect to see *films made by Christians* that

really tell the truth about God and man without conning the audience at some point or copping out at the end? I say *films made by Christians* because we have been confused by talk of Christian films, Christian music, Christian art. Why not Christian cars, Christian wheelbarrows, Christian hair shampoos? Creativity is as valid in these areas as in any other.

I would go so far as carefully to say that there is no such thing as a Christian film. There is a Christian world view and a Christian mentality, and there are Christians who are able to choose to create a film embodying these. Yet too frequently a "Christian film" is primarily an excuse for evangelism, not an expression of film as an art. Moreover, such films, disregarding film as an art form, have tended to show disrespect for man as a human being. He is often seen as an object to be evangelized, not a human being first to get alongside in unconditional love and sheer humanness.

Films today tend either to indulge the public or to hit a soft spot. *Last Tango in Paris* is an example of the former, even though some people have felt that they had been taken for a ride and that the film did not "go far enough"; *Billy Jack* is an example of the latter.

The Gospel according to St. Matthew (1966), Pier Paolo Pasolini

A film made by a Christian should do neither.

But we must face this question: Can a Christian work within the art form of the film? In view of what Bresson and Bergman, among others, have written, is it a suitable medium for a Christian? Can a Christian use the camera without distorting reality, without inducing illusion, in other words, without becoming a manipulator? In the interests of honesty, although at the risk of being discouraging, these questions should be faced.

We can, I believe, say this much. A film made by a Christian will endeavor, on the dual basis of man as created in God's image and then potentially re-created by the Holy Spirit, to declare what has truly happened to man as the result of a historical Fall. It will show the separations occasioned by this—the separation of man from God, of man from his fellows, of man from himself and of man from nature. It will show the results of these separations especially in the area of man's inhumanity to man. Shame, suffering, sin, ugliness, guilt, alienation—dialogue, images and symbols framing these concepts will be filmed. And such film will not only give insights but also show the answers to these separations, show them with truth and in humanness, beauty, love, meaning and purpose. *The Exorcist* is a case in point. The film ends in a vacuum, for the girl, although exorcised, is even more vulnerable than before, and the Christian director would indicate this and supply a biblical answer. Most directors today film the ugly things on the basis that the world as we know it is as it always was or is as God created it. But that leads to Baudelaire's conclusion: "If there is a God, he must be the Devil." On such a basis there never can be any answers.

The Christian, on the other hand, will choose to create a film that reveals a true humanness, a building of relationships and an expression of identity found through God in Christ. This task is far from easy, and all honor to those who have pioneered in this area. Its accomplishment requires an unfettered script, imaginative use of symbols and images, possibly non-professional actors, perceptive direction, handsome finance (or praying for every penny?). It may be that a director who is a Christian will have to make several films, each taking the audience further into the truth of the reality that is there, and not try to cram everything within the compass of one film.

The word *Christian* should mean something deep and profound, but through frequent misuse and gross abuse, it has come to mean too much. *Christian* means redeemed. And things, such as art forms, are redeemed only through the agency of redeemed persons. They are not necessarily redeemed just because someone who calls himself a Christian is handling them but because a redeemed thought-form and lifestyle are at work in all areas. Therefore, above all, films made by Christians will require not only totally Christian personnel but total dedication under the leadership of the Holy Spirit. The director and the producer, the actors and all involved may feel it right to ask God to do a *new* thing in cinematic thought and action, something no one has yet realized or even imagined.

christian concern, courage and compassion

What is really true of those of us who claim to be rooted in the truth, who claim to be light and salt in a world growing so dark, ugly and frightening? Are we oblivious or indifferent to the reality of man's dilemma and the reasons for it? Are we working for the best in our

culture? Are we crying for those lost in and destroying it? Do we
open our hearts and our homes in radical love to anyone who has
lost his way in the world? Is there a real demonstration that the God
of the Bible exists as we daily practice the truth in love? Do we live
by the balance of Scripture and the whole counsel of God, being
fed by the Word and filled by the Spirit? Or do we sometimes experience a failure of nerve, worried that perhaps the biblical system
cannot stand up in the marketplace of men's ideas? Each of us
should honestly answer these questions, because the more pagan
ideas and existential thinking create the cultural consensus and
monolithically surround, subsume and suffocate society, the
sharper and more isolated the Christian becomes. One of my friends
has recently been refused entry to pursue a doctoral program in a
distinguished university in the United States exclusively on the
grounds that he is a Christian.

We are approaching the situation of the first Christians where
the entire thought-forms and lifestyles that surround the Christian
are opposed to him. So do not underestimate Satan. Realize that he **115**
is the one who is behind the delusion, despair and delirium of our
day. Let us as Christians, therefore, see that we support each other
in prayer, by correspondence, by telephone and by visits, because
the crunch is coming. The Christian must go on believing God, believing that God is worthy to be believed and acting on that belief,
exerting among his contemporaries a compassionate counter-influence as he shows understanding and love for modern man who is
constantly crying out for truth, love, freedom and humanness and
is seldom finding them.

The romantic or even nihilist is one who, Gatsby-like, has his eyes
firmly fixed on the past and is stepping backwards into the future.
The Christian is confidently and lovingly to display the utter opposite of this. Aware that the times are not only disquieting but evil;
aware that God through Christ desires to make not only new people
but a new order; aware that there is no such thing as private without
public uprightness and right-standing with God; aware that there is
no such thing as "the good life" without the godly life; aware that
the coming crunch will mean increasing pressure on the Christian

as citizen in terms of personal relationships, corporate responsibilities, moral choices, aesthetic judgments, emotional tests, physical suffering and thought-stretching; aware that "where there is no vision the people perish"—aware of these, the Christian, under the leadership and empowered solely by the Holy Spirit, is still and ever to move among men and women, exerting that counter-influence, overcoming Satan by means of the blood of the Lamb, uttering his testimony and not clinging to life even when faced with persecution (Rev. 12:11).

Let us each realize the overwhelming preciousness, the surpassing worth of knowing Jesus Christ and becoming progressively more deeply and intimately acquainted with him. Let us grasp the value of perceiving, recognizing and understanding Christ more fully and clearly so that we may surely learn to sense what is vital and approve what is excellent and of real value, recognizing the highest and best and distinguishing the moral differences. May we be untainted and unerring as the day of Christ approaches, and may we abound with the fruits of right understanding and right doing which come through Jesus Christ so that his glory may be both demonstrated and recognized (Phil. 1:10 and 3:8).

I said at the beginning that it is tempting to think that cinema leads today's cultural consensus. The reader must now make up his mind. But what is difficult to deny is that in the cinema we have a miniature of the present and future rate of change that is overtaking and taking over societies in the West. The rate of speed of a film and its hurling of images at the viewer, the rich variety of technological devices available for this purpose and the statements being made— these combined give us a foretaste of the overall future. In the cinema, buttons are pressed and we respond; we are compelled to process a considerable amount of information at too rapid a pace.[9] Among other things, this results in confusion and if that continues it may result in a blurring of the essential distinction between illusion and reality.

But this is part of a chain, not an end result, that began with rationalism as expounded primarily by the Deists in the eighteenth century. Within two hundred years not only has rationalism moved

2001 (1968), Stanley Kubrick

into irrationality, but in only a decade or so it has accelerated into fantasy, neurosis and madness, the apogée of neo-romanticism. For many people today, no longer is there any reality; all is illusion, and here one makes one's own game-plan and calls that reality with the result that lifestyle becomes life.[10]

It is against such a backdrop that the Christian, with concern, courage and compassion, has to stand his ground and, having done all that the crisis demands, still stand firmly in place, knowing his calling is to be faithful not successful and, trusting in God's titanic faithfulness and not his tiny faith, practicing the truth in love.

notes

Chapter 1

[1]For those interested in the cinema as an art form, the following books are recommended: E. Lindgren, *The Art of the Film,* rev. ed. (New York: Macmillan, 1963); Ralph Stephenson and J. R. Debrix, *The Cinema As Art* (Harmondsworth: Penguin Books, 1965).

[2]Quoted in J. R. Taylor, *Cinema Eye, Cinema Ear* (New York: Hill and Wang, 1964), p. 116. Bresson uses the word *theater* for a building in which plays are performed, as distinct from a cinema where films are shown. In this book the word *cinema* is used to speak of a building but is also sometimes used as a synonym for *film.*

[3]Anyone wishing to understand how a literary script is translated into visual terms should read Ingmar Bergman's *Wild Strawberries* (London: Lorrimer Publishing, 1970). This contains the script of the film, the list of cutting continuity and a discussion on film making.

[4]In Britain at any rate theater has never been a bastard art. Invariably the great names on celluloid were first great names on the boards.

[5]Dwoskin's film *Trixi* well illustrates this. In effect, the film is the confrontation of a girl with the camera, as she reveals a complex of feelings centered around the camera.

[6]Bunuel has commented, "The film seems an involuntary imitation of dreams. The cinema might have been invented to express the life of the subconscious."

[7]From *L'Écran Français* (1948), quoted in Taylor, p. 14.

Chapter 2

[1]Today's philosophers are not so much academic as instant. The inescapable thrust of the media (whether it is a panel discussing current political issues or the matey patter of disc jockeys—the middlemen of the pop-music world) is to propagate the thought initially germinated in the universities.

[2]For a careful analysis of this and related issues, see Os Guinness, *The Dust of Death* (Downers Grove, Ill.: InterVarsity Press, 1973) and Francis A. Schaeffer, *The God Who Is There* (Downers Grove, Ill.: InterVarsity Press, 1968). I owe to Martyn Lloyd-Jones and to Francis Schaeffer a debt of gratitude for their friend-

ship and especially for the illumination that has come from their conversation and writings.

[3]Very simply, chemical determinism as propounded by Francis Crick means that man has no free will or power of choice. Psychological determinism as presented by Freud means that man is neither more nor less than a breeding animal. Both theories view man not as unique but uniform and thus fitting into a universe that operates on the assumption of the uniformity of natural causes in a closed, not open, system. See Francis A. Schaeffer, *Back to Freedom and Dignity* (Downers Grove, Ill.: InterVarsity Press, 1972).

[4]Alberto Moravia in *Man As an End* writes that "man must not suffer any more *as a means* but he must develop a new humanism, that is, he must have the courage to be a man, the centre and ultimate end of the universe."

Chapter 3

[1]In a recent interview Paul Morrissey stated that "Our [Morrissey's and Warhol's] films have always been loathed in New York because they are not a part of the main thinking of critics. But we've always had good reviews in Europe. American critics feel there's something too frivolous about our films. But what we want to do is to ridicule the importance of 'meaning.' "

[2]*Blow-Up* has the distinction of being a milestone in cinema insofar as it was "a technological breakthrough, contained ambiguities, youthful identification and arcane mystery which, along perhaps with *The Graduate,* helped to convert a generation to the postulates of the contemporary cinema."

[3]From Steve Turner, *Tonight We Will Fake Love* (London: Charisma Books, 1974).

[4]See Rollo May, *Love and Will* (New York: Norton, 1969).

Chapter 4

[1]Charlie Chaplin recalls the following remark by H. G. Wells: "There comes a moment in the day ... when you have written your pages in the morning, attended to your correspondence in the afternoon and have nothing further to do. Then comes that hour when you are bored; that's the time for sex." See N. and J. MacKenzie, *H. G. Wells* (New York: Simon and Schuster, 1973), p. 388.

[2]See Leo Madow, *Anger* (London: Allen and Unwin, 1972).

[3]For a full-scale examination of current romanticism, see Christopher Booker, *The Neophiliacs* (Glasgow: Fontana, 1970).

[4]Art and morality are not the same thing. Clive Bell has pointed out that exquisite art flourished during decadent periods in the Greek and Roman empires, in Renaissance Italy and in the French court prior to the Revolution. See Clive Bell, *Civilization* (Chicago: University of Chicago, 1973) and George Steiner, *Language and Silence* (New York: Atheneum, 1970).

[5]For an illuminating critique of this and other films by Stanley Kubrick, see Alexander Walker, *Stanley Kubrick Directs* (New York: Harcourt Brace and Jovanovich, 1972).

Chapter 6

[1]One is reminded of Stanley (in Ionesco's *Rhinoceros*) who cries that he wants to change but cannot. Surrounded by ruin and chaos, he asserts his selfhood, shouting to heaven, "Are you listening? ... I'll never give in."

Chapter 7

[1]Museum of Modern Art, Philadelphia.

Chapter 8

[1]The same criticism is to be leveled against part of a review of *The Mother and the Whore* which describes the film as "an epic of today's youth"; actually the film is a pornographic production that concerns itself with the rancidity of predatory sex.

[2]Quoted in H. Blamires, *The Christian Mind* (London: S.P.C.K., 1963), p. 101.

[3]Ibid., pp. 180-81.

[4]Another voice crying in the nihilistic wilderness is that of David Holbrook. Writing in *The Times* (London), January 4, 1974, he said, "Thinkers like Erich Fromm and Theodore Rozsak, both radicals, have warned that it is one thing to expose the morbidity of society—quite another to add to that morbidity. Other writers, like the existentialist psychotherapist Rollo May, have pointed out that such extremism causes apathy and that apathy promotes violence. . . . The masses are being taught that human beings are fit only for contempt, that man is a brute without hope and that life is pointless—while every offence to value and significance is to be applauded. The way is open for atrocities far worse than were perpetrated under Nazism, because all those values by which we feel a sense of care and concern in community have been destroyed by powerful educational influences."

[5]Writing of films in 1973, a film reviewer for *Newsweek* (January 7, 1974) said, "Never has the American screen created so many reprobates, cheats and murderers in a single year or made heroes of so many crooked cops, killers and con men. My guess is that this corrosively jaundiced atmosphere will curdle into comedy. . . . Perhaps this is more of a hope than a prophecy. . . ."

[6]See Herbert Marcuse's discussion of art as a reshaper of the nature of man in *An Essay on Liberation* (Boston: Beacon Press, 1969), pp. 37-48.

Chapter 9

[1]William Friedkin, director of *The Exorcist,* said in an interview (*Time,* February 11, 1974), "I think *The Exorcist* will be a bellwether. If it wins a wide audience, that may give the studios courage to handle more ambitious themes with more graphic scenes."

[2]See C. Stephen Evans, *Despair–A Moment or a Way of Life?* (Downers Grove, Ill.: InterVarsity Press, 1971), pp. 109-10.

[3]Mortimer J. Adler, *The Difference of Man and the Difference It Makes* (New York: World, 1968).

[4]I lean gratefully on Francis A. Schaeffer, *He Is There and He Is Not Silent* (Wheaton, Ill.: Tyndale House, 1972).

[5]See Udo Middelmann, *Pro-Existence* (Downers Grove, Ill.: InterVarsity Press, 1974), especially chapter 3.

[6]See H. R. Rookmaaker, *Modern Art and the Death of a Culture* (Downers Grove, Ill.: InterVarsity Press, 1970), especially the last chapter.

[7]John Milton, *Areopagitica: A Speech for the Liberty of Unlicensed Printing* in *Complete Poems and Major Prose,* edited by Merritt Hughes (New York: The Odyssey Press, 1957), pp. 729-30.

[8]J. Gresham Machen, "Christianity and Culture," *The Banner of Truth* (June, 1969).

[9]For an examination of this whole area, see Alvin Toffler, *Future Shock* (New York: Bantam Books, 1971).

[10]Fellini once observed, "In a sense, everything is realistic. I see no line between the imaginary and the real. I see much reality in the imaginary."